Don't Pass It On: You Can Break the Cycle

A Workbook for Mothers Who Have Struggled with Body Image, Self-Esteem, Disordered Eating, & Control

Christina E. Stai, Psy.D.

Don't Pass It On: You Can Break the Cycle

Author: Christina E. Stai

Published by Holistic Publishing

Kalona, IA 52247

holistic-publishing.com

ISBN 979-8-9855445-0-3 (paperback)

ISBN 979-8-9855445-1-0 (e-book)

ISBN 979-8-9855445-2-7 (audio)

Copyright © 2022 1st edition by Holistic Publishing

All rights reserved. No part of this publication may be reproduced, stored, or transmitted in any form or by any means—electronic, mechanical, digital, photocopy, recording, or by any other means, except as may be expressly permitted by the 1976 Copyright Act or without written permission from the author or publisher.

Printed in the United States of America

Table of Contents

Acknowledgments V

Introduction VII

Chapter 1: Pregnancy 1

Chapter 2: The Postpartum Period 17

Chapter 3: Temperament 31

Chapter 4: Infancy and the Development of Trust & Attachment 45

Chapter 5: Toddlerhood—Autonomy & Independence 65

Chapter 6: Early & Middle Childhood— the Time for Modeling,

    Initiative & Industry 79

Chapter 7: Ecological Systems 97

Chapter 8: Common Childhood Eating Habits & Concerns 109

Concluding Remarks & Statements 129

References 133

About The Author 153

Acknowledgements

The roots of this book manifested first as an appendix in my doctoral dissertation when I completed my Doctorate in Clinical Psychology at Azusa Pacific University in Southern California. My dissertation committee willingly took several years to help support and encourage me in completing my dissertation. I am exceedingly grateful to my dissertation chair, Dr. Sheryn Scott, and my other committee members, Dr. Stephen Cheung and Dr. Charity Plaxton-Hennings.

This book incorporates the work of several developmental theories. A full list of references can be found in the appendix of this book, however I would like to acknowledge a few primary theories that I incorporated extensively throughout this book. These include the work on Attachment Theory by John Bowlby, the Social Learning Theory model created by Albert Bandura, the Stages of Psychosocial Development founded by Erik Erikson, and the Ecological Systems Theory developed by Urie Bronfenbrenner.

I would like to thank my mother, Franny Girlando; mother-in-law, Rose Stai; and sister-in-law, Rebecca Stai, for doing the initial edits. I am grateful to my brother-in-law, Jeremiah Stai, for completing the design and layout of this book; and to my sister, Elanie Welch, for the hand-drawn illustrations. I am especially indebted to my husband, Josh Stai, for lighting a fire under my butt and encouraging me to finally do something with my dream to be an author. Thanks to you, that dream is now a reality.

Introduction (a.k.a. Why Should I Read This Book?)

Being a mother is hands-down one of the biggest challenges a woman will ever face in life. Beginning with pregnancy and often lasting well into the adulthood of your children, you are continuously having to shift your focus onto someone other than yourself. While most would agree that the end result is worth the effort, it goes against your very nature to selflessly give yourself to someone without any expectation of being given anything in return. Yet, this is what motherhood is all about.

During pregnancy, you sustain the life of an unborn baby by nurturing it through your own body. Then, once born, you spend every waking moment (including ones where you should be sleeping) caring for your children and making sure they have everything needed to be safe, comfortable, and content. During the first three years especially, your children are incapable of giving much of anything back to you.

This makes for a very unique relationship. In healthy adult relationships, you expect that there will always be an element of give and take. Relationships that require you to give too much without receiving anything in return ultimately dissolve. This is what makes the role of a mother so remarkable. Not only do you willingly enter into a relationship that would be unhealthy in any other context, but often you do so without a second thought about what you are sacrificing to take on this new role.

Considering how difficult it is to be a mother even when everything in life is going well, trying to tackle motherhood in the midst of more complex circumstances can feel next to impossible. There are numerous psychological difficulties that mothers, and women in general, typically face. Anxiety and depression are very common. Other challenges such as low self-esteem, poor body image, struggles with self-control (or being able to relinquish control when necessary), and disordered eating thoughts and behaviors commonly plague women. Sometimes these challenges evolve into a more serious eating disorder. Eating disorders affect three times as many women as men, and they typically develop sometime during the childbearing years. This means that there is a high likelihood that the timeframe in which a woman is working to recover from an eating disorder will also overlap with becoming a mother for the first time. The postpartum period especially tends to exacerbate struggles that were already present. The physical and hormonal changes that occur in postpartum women can heighten existing negativity around body image and can plummet self-esteem. Postpartum anxiety and depression are prevalent concerns and are even more likely to occur in women with struggles around body image, self-esteem, and disordered eating habits.

The Foundation for this Book

This book was initially inspired by my doctoral dissertation, where I examined the generational connection between mothers and daughters with eating disorders. I found that eating disorders were very commonly perpetuated from generation to generation. While many mental health conditions carry a genetic component, I couldn't help but feel that there were also a number of environmental and systemic factors contributing to the cyclical nature of these challenges. The bulk of my dissertation explored these factors in depth, and the conclusion I came to was that environmental and systemic factors greatly influence how we turn out. They shape the thoughts we have, the core values and beliefs we develop, and the way we perceive ourselves and others.

Is This Book Applicable for Me if I Don't Have an Eating Disorder?

Because my research was focused specifically on how eating disorders are perpetuated from generation to generation, you will primarily see me using eating disorders as my example throughout this book. In truth, my initial plan was to specifically target mothers with a history of eating disorders as my audience. However, as I had family and friends (who are also mothers) read through the book and help me with my initial edits, I was repeatedly told how much they resonated with large portions of this book, even though none of them had personally struggled with a full-fledged eating disorder. This encouraged me to expand my target audience and consider presenting this book as a resource for all mothers, regardless of their eating disorder history.

Therefore, while the language of this book is geared toward women who have experienced struggles with disordered eating, the initial feedback I have received tells me that there are many concepts in this book that will be very relevant to you. Most, if not all, women struggle at some point in their lives with feelings of inadequacy, low self-esteem, poor body image, difficulties with self-control, struggles with relinquishing control, depression, and/or anxiety. It is my hope that this book will be equally helpful to those who haven't had a diagnosed eating disorder as those who have. As you read through this book, I encourage you to replace the phrase "eating disorder" with your own personal struggles. You will likely find that there is a huge amount of overlap in the various challenges mothers face and that, in many ways, we are all one and the same.

Why Are New Mothers with a History of an Eating Disorder "High Risk"?

Even women who have successfully completed treatment for their eating disorder, either through outpatient therapy or a more intensive eating disorder program, may find themselves once again struggling with their eating disorder when they become pregnant or have a baby. This could happen for a number of different reasons. Most obvious is the fact that women gain weight during pregnancy. Weight gain is emotionally difficult for most women, but for those who have struggled with an eating disorder, weight gain may evoke a renewed fear of becoming fat or a fear of losing control. This fear can intensify after giving birth, especially if you then have a difficult time losing any weight you gained while pregnant.

Another common reason why many mothers struggle with their eating disorder after having a baby is the fact that babies require a lot of time, energy, and patience. If you received treatment for your eating disorder before having children, part of your treatment plan likely included taking the time for self-care. Once you have a baby, however, it can be almost impossible to have a moment to yourself. You also may be experiencing a great deal of anxiety about how to care for your newborn correctly and adequately. This can be especially challenging if you have a baby with a difficult temperament.

For these reasons and many others, you may experience resentment at times. This may scare you the first time you feel it, and then feelings of guilt for feeling resentful may follow close behind. However, it is important to know that it is perfectly ok to have these feelings. Not only has your past way of living been completely altered, but your body has changed drastically as well. Despite what you may think, you do not need to be perfect in your feelings to be a good mother. In fact, "good-enough" parenting only requires that you be "perfectly" attuned to your child less than half of the time! The concept of perfect attunement will be described in more detail later, but essentially refers to the ability to both correctly identify and appropriately meet your baby's needs in any given moment.

However, the thing that is probably the scariest of all about becoming a new mother is the thought that your eating disorder may negatively impact your children at some point in time. You have some justifiable reasons to be concerned. Eating disorders have been shown to be carried down through generations, especially between mothers and daughters. Therefore, the likelihood that your children will also struggle with disordered eating thoughts or behaviors is high. However, just because the statistics have told you one thing doesn't mean that you must sit back and accept that as an unchangeable fate.

What if I'm Not Sure if I Have an Eating Disorder?

After hearing the term, "eating disorder" thrown around so much, you may be wondering if your specific symptoms and struggles will be addressed in this book. Eating disorders manifest in a wide variety of ways, and not everyone presents with the same type or severity of symptoms. There are currently three recognized "types" of eating disorders:

- *Anorexia Nervosa*: People with Anorexia primarily engage in severe restriction of food to the point that their weight drops below 85% of what is considered their "ideal" weight. Some people with Anorexia also engage in purging behaviors to eliminate food they do consume.

- *Bulimia Nervosa*: People diagnosed with Bulimia primarily engage in a cycle involving binges, where they eat significantly more than someone would eat under "normal" circumstances, followed by purging behaviors such as vomiting, laxative use, or excessive exercise. The majority of people with Bulimia are of average weight, however they are more prone to significant weight fluctuations given the chaotic pattern of bingeing and purging.

- *Binge Eating Disorder*: People diagnosed with Binge Eating Disorder engage in periods of binge eating without any compensatory behaviors, meaning binges are not followed by purging or periods of significantly restricting food intake. People with Binge Eating Disorder are more likely to be overweight, however this is not always the case.

Not everyone fits "neatly" into one of the above diagnoses, and in fact I'd argue that most people don't fit into just one "category" or "type" of anything. Although this book cannot possibly address all aspects and nuances of disordered eating behaviors, it will apply to anyone who has struggled with some or all the following, either historically or presently:

- Fear of food and/or of gaining weight to a degree in which your everyday level of functioning is impaired. This may include things like checking your weight several times a day, or avoiding certain places— restaurants, parties, sporting events, or even rooms in your house— where you might encounter a "fear" food (a specific food you avoid because you have labeled it as "bad" or fear that consuming it will cause you to gain weight, destroy your health, etc.)

- Attempts to gain control of your weight through restricting your food intake, fasting, purging, engaging in laxative use, or participating in excessive exercise

- Experiencing a "distorted" body image. This means that the way you perceive yourself is not accurate. For example, you may think you are overweight when you are actually of average weight or underweight, or you may perceive that you have a "belly" when in fact your stomach is flat or much smaller than the average person.

- Excessive fluctuations in weight, or loss of weight to less than 85% of what is healthy for your height and age.

- Obsessive, intrusive thoughts pertaining to food or your weight that significantly impair your ability to function in your daily routine. This may include things like obsessively planning meals, being unable to stop thinking about food, or meticulously planning ways to "get rid" of unwanted weight. These obsessive thoughts occur to a degree in which they distract you from your job, schoolwork, or other important tasks.

- Symptoms of anxiety or depression may be present in reaction to thoughts of food, weight, a drive to be in control, etc. For example, you may develop intense anxiety around a certain food and turn it into a "fear" food. Or you may become depressed if you are unable to lose the weight you want to or if your body doesn't look the way you want it to.

- Obsessive or rigid adherence to following a specific diet or eating plan in the absence of any known food allergies/sensitivities or health conditions that would otherwise indicate necessity for following a strict diet. This may include things like rigidly tracking macronutrients, cutting out an entire food group (such as refusing to eat anything with gluten, refined sugars, etc.) or severely restricting or eliminating foods that are not organic, non-GMO, or otherwise considered "healthy."

The final bullet point is speaking to a growing phenomenon that has emerged within Western culture and is especially prevalent in the United States. Diets such as Paleo, Ketogenic, and Whole30 are growing in popularity. While the intention of these eating styles is to increase awareness around the importance of taking care of your body and knowing what you are putting into your body, unfortunately many people are taking these diets to the extreme. There are now enough people struggling with rigidity around these diets that a new eating disorder diagnosis, called "Orthorexia," has been proposed.

Do I Need to be in Therapy or Have Gone Through Formal Treatment to Effectively Use This Book?

The short answer to this is: No. You can use this book however you want, and it is designed to offer practical ways to make changes and shift behaviors if you are willing and able to make those changes. That being said, change is difficult, and cycles are hard to break. People tend to experience more success when they have a support system backing them. For some people, having a loving group of friends or family members may be enough. Many others, however, find they are better able to meet their goals and maintain health and wellness when they have a treatment team to support them as well. Your treatment team may consist of any combination of therapists, medication prescribers, medical doctors, dietitians, nutritionists, personal trainers, coaches, spiritual mentors, etc. I mention therapists and dietitians/nutritionists very often throughout this book because, in my personal and professional experience, having an established relationship with these providers is often the key to long-term recovery and maintenance of whatever mental health struggles you may be facing.

How to Use This Book

This book is laid out in developmental order, beginning with pregnancy, and ending with experiences you may have as your children reach middle childhood. Each chapter focuses on a different aspect of motherhood and how your eating disorder may be impacted during your child's various developmental stages. One of the purposes of the book is to provide you with some education surrounding what to expect during each developmental stage. However, you do not need to read this book in any specific order. You may have children at various ages and developmental stages, so you should feel free to skip around and focus on the sections that are most applicable for you and your children at this particular time.

In addition to the educational piece presented in each chapter, you will find sections entitled, "Reflections," "Application," and "Narratives." The Reflections section contains excerpts that will allow you to more deeply process what comes up for you. There may be some things you elect to discuss later with your therapist or a trusted loved one. The Application section is designed to give you some practical ideas and tangible ways to implement what you learn. While likely helpful for any mother, the activities in this section are specifically tailored to the unique needs that you will have as a mother who has battled an eating disorder. The Narratives section will give you illustrated examples of some of the ways women may struggle to balance motherhood with recovery at each developmental stage. While the narratives are entirely fictional, they are designed to be raw and realistic. Some of what you read may resonate with you. The stories may also trigger you or bring up strong feelings of judgment, criticism, etc. For that reason, it is recommended that you have someone to process this section with, such as a therapist, partner, or close friend.

Each chapter of this book is relatively short and, if you wanted to, you could probably read it in its entirety within a day or two. However, I strongly encourage you to take your time with this book. It is designed to be much more than a quick read that functions as a simple source of information. Its deeper purpose is to confront your concepts of both motherhood and your eating disorder and to allow you to utilize these challenges to your existing beliefs constructively.

For that reason, I would ask you to treat this book as more of an interactive workbook than anything else. It is meant to be used along with a separate notebook, so you have ample space to reflect on and sort through what comes up for you in each chapter. The Reflections and Narratives sections have some specific prompts to help guide this process for you, but do not feel limited by those prompts. Rather, use them as a scaffold to expand and build on the inner work you are doing. Take a few days, or even a week or two, to really sit with the content in each chapter before moving on to the next chapter. If you are working with a therapist, you may elect to use your scheduled sessions to help pace yourself. For example, if you see your therapist once a week, plan to spend at least a week on each chapter and then use your therapy sessions as a space to unpack everything you've processed.

Journaling allows you to put your thoughts and feelings into words, and symbolically that can help you let go of things more easily because, instead of circulating around in your brain for eternity, your thoughts now have a "home" on the pages of your notebook. This helps your brain relax because it is no longer responsible for remembering anything. This is a wonderful thing, especially for those of you who tend to be on the anxious or obsessive side.

Journaling can also be a great way to measure your progress as you do the work on yourself. The healing journey is just that—a journey. And, often, that journey can feel like it is taking a lot longer than you'd like it to. Forward progress is frequently very slow, and that can evoke frustration, impatience, and discouragement. However, imagine going back and re-reading a journal entry that you made 6 months ago. Chances are good that a lot of things will have changed in that time period. So, while you may perceive the day-to-day progress as slow going, your overall growth is what matters most. Journaling gives you an opportunity to see the bigger picture of your healing journey, instead of just focusing on the tiny details.

Above all else, this book is designed to be used as a tool to utilize in your own healing journey. My hope is that it offers you encouragement and support, and that it provides you with a feeling of empowerment as you navigate this special yet challenging time in your life. I am optimistic that it will not only be a resource for you as you learn to simultaneously balance caring for your children and progressing in your recovery (from whatever it is you need to recover from), but that it will be a respite for you during stressful times as well. I anticipate you will learn many things that you didn't know about child development, and as a result you may make the choice to alter some of your behaviors. However, the point of this book is not to change you or single out all the things you're doing wrong as a mother. Rather, it is meant to embolden you and give you renewed hope for being the mother you know you can be.

Chapter 1: Pregnancy

Chapter 1: Pregnancy

Pregnancy is often spoken about in overly positive ways. It's common to hear people talk about how they can tell a woman is pregnant because of the way she "glows," and we're bombarded with fantasy-like social media pictures of smiling parents-to-be proudly gazing down at the woman's growing belly. While these times do exist for many people, for women who have gone through or who are still battling an eating disorder or other mental health condition, pregnancy can be a fearful and emotionally trying time. Pregnancy is an important time for you to keep your eating habits healthy and in control not just for yourself, but for the life that resides inside of you as well.

Inevitably, you will be given guidelines about healthy weight gain. This can be a huge trigger if you have ever engaged in disordered eating behaviors, because during that time you likely spent a lot of time finding ways to control your weight. The weight you gain may radically alter your physical appearance, and it won't just be limited to your growing belly. Stretch marks appear, breasts get larger, feet swell up, and faces become fuller. Your changing body means a change in hormones too. It is common for women to experience a shift in mood during pregnancy, with many reporting periods of being overly emotional or reactive.

You may also be requested or required to discontinue many (if not all) psychotropic medications you may be taking. This means that, during one of the most emotionally challenging and relapse-prone times you'll face in your life, you'll be forced to rely on whatever coping skills and other available supports and resources you've developed along the way, without the assistance of medical stabilization.

It is certainly possible to make it through this time, and many women who have struggled with disordered eating and other mental health conditions go on to successfully make it through one or more pregnancies without experiencing a relapse. However, it is essential to acknowledge and validate that this will be a trying time for many and that struggles, slips, and relapses are common. Because of this, your pregnancy will be an important time to ensure you have an adequate social and emotional support system in place.

Those who engage in disordered eating behaviors during pregnancy are more likely to see adverse results. Some research has indicated that babies born to mothers who are engaged in their eating disorder during pregnancy have more physical challenges, are smaller, and weigh less than those born to mothers without an eating disorder. This makes sense biologically, because if you are depriving yourself of much needed nutrients during your pregnancy, then you're also depriving your unborn baby of these nutrients. If babies don't get what they need, then they won't grow as quickly as those who are being provided with the necessary nutrition.

The combination of the physical and emotional challenges of pregnancy, along with the risks that come with engaging in an eating disorder while pregnant, makes this time particularly tricky. On the one hand, slips can be justified given the circumstances. On the other hand, serious negative consequences could impact the development of your child as a result of any slips or relapses. Therefore, the amount of grace you give yourself must be weighed against the negative outcomes that could occur.

One thing that may help you navigate this precarious time is to shift your focus onto your unborn baby. Many women who struggle with an eating disorder have a hard time doing something for their own benefit. However, if you concentrate on the life that is growing inside of you, you will likely experience a stronger drive to do what needs to be done to keep both yourself and your baby healthy. Reframe the weight you're gaining as nutrition, energy, and protection that you are providing for your baby. View your body, not as your own, but as the safe space that you are providing to help your baby stay strong and healthy. This won't work any miracles in your thinking, but shifting your focus onto someone else's needs often helps to diminish the perceived importance of your own wants.

Morning Sickness

Morning sickness is a common "side effect" of pregnancy, especially in the first trimester, and it occurs in upwards of 70% of all pregnancies. For most people, morning sickness is unpleasant yet mostly tolerable. However, for anyone who has struggled with an eating disorder, morning sickness can be a complicated experience.

Women with a history of Anorexia or restrictive eating habits may find themselves slipping into increased restrictive behaviors. While this will likely begin as an attempt to mitigate symptoms of nausea or vomiting, the risk for it evolving into more of a disordered eating presentation is very high. It is common for women to experience an aversion to certain specific foods when they are experiencing morning sickness, however it is important to distinguish this from an active avoidance of a food for other reasons, such as fear of weight gain or wanting an excuse to not have to eat a "fear" food. For example, if you had previously restricted sugar when you were most active in your eating disorder and have since gotten to a place in your recovery where you allow yourself to eat dessert after dinner most nights, you may find yourself experiencing an urge to restrict desserts again and to justify that restriction based on your morning sickness. For this reason, it is very important that you are fully honest with yourself and your healthcare providers during this time.

Those with a history of Bulimia who primarily engaged in vomiting as their purging behavior may be triggered if they experience episodes of vomiting due to morning sickness. Some studies have suggested that women with a history of Bulimia are more likely to experience genuine morning sickness during their pregnancy. However, it is also likely that you may experience a stronger urge to engage in purging behaviors in the absence of morning sickness during this time, especially since it can easily be disguised by labeling it as morning sickness. Here again, it will be crucial for you to be fully honest both with yourself and your healthcare team when it comes to distinguishing between true symptoms of your pregnancy vs. a recurrence of disordered eating thoughts or behaviors.

Because of the likelihood of some overlap between morning sickness and the way it may trigger or increase urges to engage in disordered eating behaviors, it is highly recommended that you work with a dietician or nutritionist during this time. They will be able to help you get the appropriate amount of nutrients in your body for your baby, and they will also likely be able to give you some guidance on how best to structure mealtimes, amounts, and the kinds of foods to eat to mitigate symptoms of morning sickness. Depending on the severity of your morning sickness, it also may be recommended that you take medication to decrease episodes of vomiting, especially if there is concern that you are not retaining enough nutrients to adequately nourish yourself and your baby.

Food Cravings

Another very common pregnancy symptom involves a craving for specific foods. Between 50% – 90% of women in the United States report experiencing food cravings during their pregnancy. Most commonly, food cravings begin in the first trimester, peak in the second trimester, and decline during the third trimester. While pregnant women can have a craving for any food, the most common include sweets, dairy, starchy carbohydrates, fruits, vegetables, and fast food.

Looking at that list itself may be enough to trigger someone who's struggled with an eating disorder, but the trigger can manifest in really different ways depending on your own personal experience. For those who have experienced times of bingeing, many of these foods are popular "binge foods." If this has been your experience, it will be important for you to monitor your cravings and your intake, and particularly to not use your cravings as a justification to binge (or to binge and then purge). This does not mean that you shouldn't ever eat a food you are craving, only that you'll need to regulate your intake, just like you would with any previous binge food. The main difference now is recognizing that your cravings may be stronger and are more hormonally driven because of your pregnancy.

In contrast, for those who have engaged in restrictive behaviors, you may label many of the things on this list as a "fear food." Developing a craving for a fear food may be both confusing and terrifying for you. Here, too, it will be crucial to monitor your tendency to restrict or deny yourself of the foods that you are craving and be honest with yourself and your healthcare team about any urges you have to engage in your eating disorder. It is highly encouraged that you continue to work with a dietitian or nutritionist throughout your entire pregnancy, but especially during the times when food cravings are highest, as this will most likely be the time when urges to engage in your eating disorder will also be high.

Miscarriage

Between 10-15% of known pregnancies in the United States end in a miscarriage. Most miscarriages occur before 12 weeks' gestation, however up to 5% of miscarriages occur between 13 – 19 weeks' gestation. Miscarriages can happen for several reasons, and to this day the cause of most miscarriages remains unknown.

Women who experience a miscarriage tend to experience a wide range of emotions. Sadness, grief, and guilt are all very common. It is important to reiterate that, for the vast majority of pregnancies that result in miscarriage, there was nothing that you did to cause the miscarriage, and there is nothing you could have done differently to have had a different result. Some women may also experience feelings of relief, even if their pregnancy was wanted or planned. This is very normal and is nothing to be ashamed of. It is also very common to experience anxiety after a miscarriage, with many women developing a fear of having another miscarriage.

It is important to remember that these numbers are true regardless of whether or not you've struggled with an eating disorder. The vast majority of women who are in recovery from an eating disorder have no significant differences in pregnancy outcomes than women who have no eating disorder history. However, women who are actively engaging in an eating disorder during their pregnancy may be at a greater risk of miscarrying than those who are not currently active in their eating disorder. An unborn baby is more likely to experience fetal distress if you are not eating enough to adequately sustain the baby, or if you are regularly engaging in significant purging behaviors. Some research suggests that women struggling with Bulimia are more likely to experience a miscarriage than women with other types of eating disorders. However, it's important to emphasize that active engagement in any type of eating disorder can cause fetal distress. This is why it is so important to seek professional help if you are struggling with controlling your eating disorder while pregnant.

Stillbirth

While much rarer than miscarriage, about 1 in 160 (.006 %) pregnancies in the United States result in stillbirth. Similar to miscarriage, the cause of stillbirth is still widely unknown. However, women who are actively engaging in an eating disorder during their pregnancy have been shown to have a higher risk for stillbirth than those who have never had an eating disorder and those who have an eating disorder history but are not currently engaging in their eating disorder.

Like miscarriage, the emotions experienced with a stillbirth are typically complex and multifaceted. In addition to the grief you experience from losing a child, you are also still left with all of the physical and medical aftermath of having carried a baby to term. For women with an eating disorder history, this can be especially challenging. Your body will show the "marks" of being pregnant, and it may feel like those bodily changes are all that is left after your hard work to take care of yourself and your baby and to manage your eating disorder. The combination of grief and having a drastically changed physical appearance may significantly increase your risk for relapse, so this is an especially crucial time to seek out professional help and to utilize other sources of support you have around you.

Reflections

Think about which aspect of your pregnancy has been the most challenging in your recovery from your eating disorder. Some women may struggle most with the fact that they are gaining weight. Others may become anxious about the focus they have to put on the food they have consumed that day and whether or not the amount and content are enough to keep both themselves and their baby healthy. Still others may be battling intense fluctuations in emotions, the results of which may lead to negative thoughts and feelings about themselves or their baby.

What has been your biggest personal struggle? Whatever it is that you are experiencing, it is important that you communicate this to your therapist and others within your support system. Remember that there is nothing shameful about struggling with your eating disorder during your pregnancy, and that being able to voice your struggles is a sign of strength, not weakness.

After acknowledging where your struggles are, take some time to think about your unborn baby. What and who do you think they will look like? What are you most looking forward to about being a mother? How do you envision your relationship with your baby?

Application

Sometimes when people are in the midst of an intense struggle, it can be difficult to think about anything else. Yet the ability to shift your focus onto something or someone else oftentimes enables you to get out of your own "stuff" and stop the "spinning hamster wheel" that at times takes over your brain. Taking the time to think about your unborn baby allows you the opportunity to begin the attachment relationship while they are still in the womb. The more attached you feel to your baby, the easier it will be for you to do the things you need to do, such as eating right and gaining weight to keep your baby healthy.

Pregnancy can be a very surreal experience. You may logically understand that there is a life growing inside of you, and as your pregnancy goes on you will begin to feel it physically as well. On the other hand, you are making an attempt to develop a relationship with an unknown, intangible being. This can make it difficult to feel as though you are creating an attachment to your unborn baby. As will be detailed in later chapters, mothers who have suffered with an eating disorder are at higher risk of having children with an insecure attachment. Pregnancy is an opportune time to begin developing the parent-child relationship, because your baby is always there with you. If you are struggling to connect with your baby, or are looking to grow an already established connection, try the following:

1. Take the time to talk to, read stories, or sing to your baby. This will help your baby get to know your voice better, and it will give you a way to start connecting on an emotional level. Rubbing or hugging your belly can help build this connection as well.

2. When you eat, talk to your baby about what you are eating and how it will help with growth and development. This will also likely decrease your own anxiety around eating, because now you will be focused on how it is benefitting your baby rather than what you perceive it may be doing to you.

3. Take time to learn about the development of your baby while you are pregnant. There are several apps available where you can track along with the growth and changes that are happening for your baby week by week until you deliver. This will give you a more tangible way to connect with your baby, because you'll be able to track along day by day with how much your baby is growing, what body parts are developing, etc.

Narratives

Amy is single and 14 weeks pregnant with her first child. Her pregnancy was unplanned and although she has chosen to maintain the pregnancy, she has struggled with ambivalent feelings and is finding it difficult to connect with her baby. Amy has struggled with an intense desire to be in control for most of her life. This need for control oftentimes manifested in the way in which she controlled her food intake.

As a child, Amy recalled obsessing over certain foods, for example only eating foods of a certain color or size. As a teenager, this evolved into severe restriction around how much she ate, where she would decrease her food intake more and more to see how little she could eat in a day. As a young adult, this led to a period of over-exercise as well. This continued until it began to interfere with her grades in college, because she was spending more time working out than doing her homework.

Amy began working with a therapist who helped her identify some of her core beliefs around control, and she began to understand why control was such an important issue for her. With ongoing support from her therapist and a few close friends, Amy was drastically able to loosen up and reduce her need for control.

However, Amy's surprise pregnancy was very stressful for her, and her anxiety and urge for control increased significantly. She again began obsessing over what foods she ate and how many calories she was consuming to ensure her baby was getting enough but to also mitigate how much weight she gained. Amy began to resent her baby for disrupting her life, and the thought of how much more her life would change after the baby's birth made her anxiety skyrocket.

Sarah is married and pregnant with her third child. Her other children are 5 and 2. Sarah has struggled off and on with binge eating for most of her life, combined at times with purging behaviors to try and "off-set" some of the binges she went on. Sarah has not engaged in any purging behaviors for 6 years but continues to struggle with bingeing and emotional eating. Sarah has gained more weight in her current pregnancy than she did in her previous 2 pregnancies combined.

This substantial weight gain has not gone unnoticed by friends and family, many of whom have made snide remarks to Sarah or have talked amongst themselves behind her back. This has caused Sarah to feel discouraged and alone, which has also increased her urge to eat to help herself feel better.

Sarah has found herself using her pregnancy as an excuse to eat whatever she wants whenever she wants, even though she knows this is not healthy for her recovery.

Sarah is also struggling to feel connected to her baby. It has been harder for her to differentiate between her excess weight and the natural growth of her belly as her pregnancy progresses. This baby is also much less active than her first two were, and the lack of movement in her belly further disconnects her and at times she finds herself almost forgetting that she is pregnant.

Michelle is a dietician. She is 30 weeks pregnant with her second child and has an 11-year-old daughter. During her first pregnancy, Michelle was just a teenager and didn't know what she was doing or how to take care of herself. She regularly drank alcohol and smoked marijuana until she learned she was pregnant at about 8 weeks. She then stopped using substances for the duration of her pregnancy, but her eating habits remained poor and consisted primarily of fast-food and quick meals of mainly processed foods.

When she was born, Michelle's daughter struggled with a lot of health issues, including some food allergies which went undiagnosed until she was 5 years old. After giving birth, Michelle became a vegetarian and started eating low- and non-fat foods to try and lose her "baby weight." Her daughter was diagnosed as being lactose intolerant when she was 6 months old, so Michelle then became vegan.

Since receiving her training, Michelle has struggled with varying degrees of Orthorexia. After her daughter received a diagnosis of Celiac Disease when she was 5, Michelle elected to start eating meat products again and tried out a Paleo diet. She then became interested in the Keto diet and started meticulously tracking her macronutrients. She eliminated all processed foods, sugars, and artificial flavorings and colors.

Since becoming pregnant with her second child, Michelle's anxiety has significantly increased, and she has been having nightmares and intrusive thoughts about her next child having similar health issues. Michelle began buying only organic products and has cut out all possible allergens, now rigidly following an autoimmune protocol diet even though she herself does not have any known food allergies or substantial food sensitivities. She does not go out to eat and rarely goes over to friends' houses for events unless she can be sure they will have food she can eat.

Spend some time reflecting on the narratives you just read and identify what comes up for you. Think about what does and doesn't resonate with you. Pay attention to your inner monologue and be honest about things you read that cause you to judge or criticize the women in these narratives. Also, be mindful of anything that triggers you. It is recommended that you utilize your journal to process this section of each chapter more fully.

Chapter 2:
The Postpartum Period

Chapter 2: The Postpartum Period

The time period immediately following giving birth can be wrought with a variety of conflicting thoughts and emotions. There is likely a large part of you that is overjoyed with the arrival of the miracle you helped create. However, after 9 months of anticipation, the aftermath of giving birth can sometimes leave you with the same feeling you get after a holiday or vacation is over. You spent so much of your time and energy looking toward what was ahead, but once you're finally there, reality can hit hard. Once the excitement has worn off, extended family has left, and your partner, if you have one, has gone back to work, it can sometimes feel like you're in this by yourself. Many women feel this way, but if you've also struggled with an eating disorder or other mental health condition at some point in your life, this time can be very difficult.

Your experience with labor and delivery can have a significant impact on your postpartum recovery as well. This is especially true if your labor or delivery didn't go the way you had hoped or planned. For example, if you wanted to have a "natural" childbirth without the use of any medication or interventions, you may be struggling if you ended up getting an epidural or having a C-Section. If there were any medical complications that required surgery or an extended hospital stay for either you or your baby, understandably that can further increase feelings of disappointment, stress, depression, and anxiety.

One obvious challenge faced explicitly by mothers who have suffered from an eating disorder is the anxiety that surrounds body weight and eating habits. If you were struggling in these areas before or during your pregnancy, then your chance of feeling distressed in the weeks after giving birth is higher. This high level of distress has been linked to higher rates of Postpartum Depression and Postpartum Anxiety.

Postpartum Depression

Between 70% – 80% of women experience what is referred to as, "Baby Blues," and between 10% - 20% of women meet criteria for Postpartum Depression. The onset of Postpartum Depression presents within the first four weeks after delivering your baby and can be recognized by the following symptoms:

- Feeling depressed most of the time

- Decreased pleasure in things you used to enjoy

- Changes in appetite or significant weight gain or loss

- Sleep disturbance (insomnia, hypersomnia)

- Agitation, lack of energy, or fatigue

- Intense feelings of guilt or worthlessness

- Difficulty concentrating or making decisions

- Frequently occurring thoughts of death or suicide

- Difficulty attaching to, or feeling love for your baby

Several symptoms of Postpartum Depression overlap with the natural after-effects of pregnancy. It's expected that after you deliver your baby, you will experience at least some shift in eating and sleeping habits, because now you are having to take care of a baby in addition to taking care of your own needs. It goes without saying that you will feel more fatigued, because chances are good that you're up at all hours of the day and night to feed your baby.

You also may experience a very natural shift in interests and pleasures, because you are now taking on a new role as "Mother," and an expected consequence of that role is that your priorities will change. Sometimes it can be difficult to decipher whether you're truly suffering from Postpartum Depression or whether you're just experiencing an expected lifestyle change. If you think that you may be suffering from Postpartum Depression, then it is important that you communicate this to your therapist or doctor so they can help you to best manage your symptoms.

The Postpartum Depression symptom that tends to elicit the most concern for new mothers is the experience of struggling to feel emotionally attached to or experience love for your baby. This is exacerbated by the very high expectation that the second your baby is born, you will feel an overwhelming unconditional love. That is a very real experience for a lot of new mothers, but it absolutely is not a universal experience. If you are suffering from Postpartum Depression, it is very common that there will be periodic, or more consistent, periods of time where you find it very difficult to connect with your baby. The truth is that your baby is not going to be very interactive with you in the first several weeks of life, and for some women, that lack of emotional and social interaction makes it hard to connect with their baby. Your sole purpose in those first several weeks is to keep your baby fed and change their diapers. This is not a glamorous job by any means, and you may be doing a lot of it by yourself, especially if your partner is working fulltime, if you are a single mom, or if you don't have extended family or friends nearby to help out. You may have times where you don't feel love toward your baby, and you may even experience resentment, anger, or hatred.

It is critical to emphasize that if you ever experience intrusive thoughts of wanting to harm your baby, it is crucial that you speak to your doctor or therapist right away, as this could mean you are suffering from Postpartum

Psychosis. This is a very rare condition, impacting only about 1-2 women out of 1,000. Unfortunately, up to 10% of cases of Postpartum Psychosis result in suicide or infanticide. Fortunately, Postpartum Psychosis is very treatable with a combination of medication and therapy. Most women experience a complete remission of symptoms in as little as 2 weeks. It's important to note that Postpartum Psychosis is completely separate from other psychotic disorders such as Schizophrenia, and if you do experience Postpartum Psychosis, this does not mean you are psychotic or that you will develop a chronic severe psychotic disorder. Most of the time, treatment will be short-term, meaning you will not need to be on medication for a significant period of time, typically not more than a few months to a year.

Research indicates that that up to 70% of women who are actively engaging in their eating disorder during pregnancy suffer from Postpartum Depression after giving birth. In contrast, those who have a history of an eating disorder but are not actively engaging in behaviors during their pregnancy suffer from Postpartum Depression 30% of the time. That's a big difference, and by making the choice to not engage in eating-disordered behavior during your pregnancy, you are likely decreasing your chances of experiencing Postpartum Depression as well. Of course, as evidenced by the previous chapter on pregnancy, that choice may not always be the easiest one to make. The bottom line, however, is that if you are suffering from Postpartum Depression, you are not alone.

Now you know that the postpartum period can put you at risk for depression and isolation. If you were previously working, then you're probably on maternity leave for at least 6 weeks. Depending on how your delivery went, you may be unable to be very active. To top it all off, you now have a tiny person to take care of as well. The combination of these things can be overwhelming and can put you at a greater risk of relapsing in your eating disorder, so it will be essential for you to continue receiving support from your healthcare team to decrease your chances of fully relapsing into your eating disorder.

Postpartum Anxiety

Postpartum Anxiety unfortunately has not been studied nearly as much as Postpartum Depression has, despite numerous studies now indicating that Postpartum Anxiety is more common than Postpartum Depression. Some research indicates that up to about 28% of women experience some form of Postpartum Anxiety, which may consist of the following symptoms:

- Persistent worrying about your baby

- Feelings of dread about things that might happen to your baby

- Sleep disturbance (separate from waking to feed and care for a newborn)

- Racing thoughts

- Heart palpitations

- Hyperventilation

- Shakiness or trembling

- Panic attack symptoms (racing heart, dizziness, feeling like you can't breathe, are having a heart attack, or are going to die)

Like Postpartum Depression, Postpartum Anxiety is more likely to occur if you have a history of an eating disorder, or if you have struggled with anxiety or other mental health issues in the past. Other factors that can increase your chances for Postpartum Anxiety include having a history of mood swings during your menstrual cycle, as well as having experienced a miscarriage or stillbirth. It's also hard to ignore the very real and scary warning of Sudden Infant Death Syndrome (SIDS) that is plastered all over many of the items you now own. While SIDS is extremely rare (around 1,300 SIDS cases/year in the US), it does happen, and it is still largely unknown why.

At the root of any anxiety disorder is a fear of being out of control, and that inherent drive to get back in control can be a prime catalyst for re-engaging in disordered eating or other unhelpful coping skills. You may try to over-control your baby's environment, including who and what you allow to be around or in the house, and what types of clothing, bedding, toys, etc. you use. Again, this is why having a support system that includes a therapist and family/friends to talk to is so important. You will need someone to whom you can go to share your anxieties and fears without judgment but who will also be able to help you see things from a rational place.

Breastfeeding

The choice to breastfeed is a very personal one, and in some cases it may be out of your control (such as if you have a low milk supply or your baby struggles to latch). If you want to breastfeed but are struggling for any reason, don't be afraid or embarrassed about asking for help. Many hospitals have lactation consultants who can help show you some strategies to nurse more successfully. Many doulas and midwives are also trained in lactation, so they would also be a great resource. It is important to remember that it is very common for women to have difficulties with breastfeeding. Especially if this is your first baby, it would be helpful to remind yourself that you've never done this before, so it's ok if you don't know how to do it correctly!

It's also important to note that the notion that *all* women can breastfeed is highly inaccurate. Some women will never be able to breastfeed successfully, often due to a persistent low milk supply (sometimes called primary lactation failure) that is caused by a condition called Insufficient Glandular Tissue (IGT) or Mammary Hypoplasia. This occurs when there is not enough mammary tissue that developed in adolescence, which is needed to be able to support milk production. There may also be something going on with your baby that makes nursing difficult or unsuccessful. One of the most common reasons why babies struggle to latch is due to having a tongue tie, which is when a band of tissue anchors their tongue to the bottom of their mouth. Some babies with tongue ties have no issues, but it can impact breastfeeding, eating, and speaking. A simple and quick surgical procedure can be performed to correct the tongue tie if there are long-term issues.

For those who choose to breastfeed, it is important to be aware of things that may trigger you to engage in your eating disorder. For example, you may feel an urge to eat or avoid certain things because you've been told eating that thing will either benefit or harm your baby. It is true that some of the nutrients you consume pass through your breast milk to your baby, and it is true you should be mindful to a degree about what you eat. However, for someone with a history of an eating disorder, this is a slippery slope that can easily escalate if you aren't being mindful and aware of what is going on for you.

Self-Care

One of the best things you can do to manage your own and your baby's well-being is being proactive and coming up with some ideas about what will help you feel supported, stay connected, and pass the time during the first 6-8 weeks post-delivery. Many new mothers neglect self-care. While motherhood often requires you to put your child's needs above your own, it does not require you to abandon your needs altogether. In fact, doing so will impair your ability to parent effectively because, as you've likely learned from your own treatment and therapy, it's hard to be available to meet the needs of someone else fully when your own emotional resources are depleted. A lack of self-care will also model for your children that they are not supposed to respect or value themselves and their own needs as much as they value the needs of others. Motherhood is about finding the balance between getting your child's needs met while also finding the time to have yours met.

Reflections

1. What are your biggest concerns about motherhood?

2. What are your biggest concerns about your eating disorder recovery and/or your recovery from other mental health conditions?

3. Have you experienced symptoms of Postpartum Depression? Which ones?

4. Have you experienced symptoms of Postpartum Anxiety? Which ones?

5. What has your feeding experience been like? How does it compare to the ideas (or ideals) you had about it prior to your baby being born? What emotions are being brought up for you around breastfeeding, pumping, formula, etc.?

Application

This chapter emphasized the importance of finding time to take care of yourself in the midst of caring for your new infant. Now it's time to do something to ensure that you get this time in. Use the following list to help get you started, then create a list of these and other ideas, along with possible days/times when you can commit to doing these things. You are much more likely to follow through on something if you make a specific plan to do it.

- Do you have friends or relatives who live nearby and have flexible work hours who could come spend time with you and/or help around the house and with your baby?

- Do you have friends or relatives who live farther away but could be available via Zoom or Facetime?

- What are some simple things outside of the house that you enjoy that could be manageable while taking your infant with you or leaving them with a friend or family member for an hour or so (grabbing a cup of coffee, getting your nails or hair done, visiting a bookstore, going to see a movie, receiving a post-pregnancy massage)?

- Is it possible for you to schedule additional sessions with your therapist during this time, so you have some extra support?

Narratives

Linda has been in recovery from Anorexia for two years. She just came home with her newborn. She had a long, difficult labor and delivery that resulted in a C-section. While her baby is healthy, Linda's recovery has been slow and painful. Because she has been in so much pain, she has struggled with the patience to breastfeed, so she has been primarily formula-feeding her baby. Linda feels a lot of guilt for doing this, as she had envisioned breastfeeding her baby as the "perfect" way to bond with her baby. Linda is struggling not to dwell on all the "advice" she's been given about how her baby won't attach to her properly if she doesn't breastfeed, and she also worries about not being able to give her baby the "perfect" nutrition. The lack of control Linda had over her delivery and her ability to breastfeed has stirred up her drive to be in control over everything else, something she hasn't experienced since she was most active in her eating disorder over 2 years ago. Linda is finding herself becoming overly rigid about her infant's feeding times, to the point where she is meticulously tracking what time her infant feeds and how much is eaten at each feeding. If the time interval or amount is off in any way, Linda becomes extremely anxious that her baby won't get what it needs and won't grow appropriately.

Maria had periods of bingeing and restricting, which resulted in significant weight fluctuations, however her eating habits have never gotten out of control to the point of needing significant therapeutic interventions. Maria had what she would consider a "perfect" labor and delivery with her second child. There were no complications, and she was able to deliver her baby vaginally with a relatively short labor and the help of an epidural, which Maria had planned to have. Maria has chosen to breastfeed her baby, and this is going smoothly. Her baby is also an excellent sleeper. Because of all of this, Maria is confused and scared when she begins experiencing symptoms of Postpartum Depression. She is struggling to feel connected to her infant, even during feeding times. Instead, she finds herself daydreaming about the time in her life before she had kids and could do whatever she wanted. She becomes more frightened when these thoughts evolve into passive suicidal ideation, which includes wishing she was no longer in her current life. Maria begins to find comfort in food and uses that as a way to cope. She finds herself struggling to control her eating and begins having times of binge eating several times a week.

Ashley has struggled with severe anxiety and Orthorexia for the past 10 years. Her pregnancy was unexpected and came just a few weeks after she had a miscarriage at 12 weeks with her first child. Although her baby is healthy, Ashley's delivery with her second child was traumatic for her. During delivery, it was discovered that the umbilical cord was wrapped around the baby's neck, and Ashley had to delivery her baby quickly so the doctors could unwrap the cord and help the baby breathe. Ashley's baby was not breathing initially and had to be hooked up to oxygen for a few hours, however after that has been doing fine and has had no other issues. Despite this, Ashley is struggling to get past the trauma of the birth and finds herself going into a panic several times a day because she has a sudden "feeling" that her baby is no longer breathing. Ashley has started fixating on the possibility of SIDS and spends hours a day researching everything she can about how to prevent SIDS. She has significantly altered her diet and the way in which she feeds her baby, all in an attempt to ensure her baby stays healthy and develops strong lungs. If she doesn't follow her new diet exactly, Ashley berates herself for her lack of control.

Spend time reflecting on and journaling about the above narratives. Was there anything you read that triggered you? Which person did you find you most identified with? Who did you feel the most amount of judgment toward?

Chapter 3: Temperament

Chapter 3: Temperament

All newborns are difficult to take care of at one point or another, but each infant is difficult in different areas. As a new mother, you can do your best to prepare yourself for what is to come, but you'll never really know what your child is like until they are born. This is where the concept of temperament comes in. Temperament is how we describe our basic human nature and how we behave in the world. As we all know, no two people are alike, and we're all impacted by a combination of our genes and our environment.

While our environment undoubtedly will impact us and our personality development throughout our lives, temperament is considered to be relatively stable and permanent. That means that children with a more "difficult" temperament typically grow into difficult-tempered adults, and children with an "easy-going" temperament grow into adults who have that same temperament. The more you're able to learn about your child and their own unique temperament, the easier it will be to parent that child. While you're discovering what your child's temperament is like, it would also be helpful for you to examine yourself and figure out what kind of temperament you have. Once you know what your and your child's temperaments are like, you can be more proactive in how you relate and react toward your children.

The theory of temperament began to be explored in the 1950s by two psychologists, Alexander Thomas and Stella Chess. They conducted many studies for several decades, most of which were longitudinal, meaning they followed a group of participants for several years to track development and changes. Through their research, they identified three categories of temperament that babies tend to fall under: easy (flexible), difficult (feisty), and slow to warm (fearful).

Easy and flexible babies are typically happy, engaging, predictable, and content. They are able to go with the flow and can tolerate changes in their schedule pretty well. It is estimated that about 40% of babies fit into this category. Difficult and feisty infants are unpredictable, easily irritated, intensely emotional, and are hard to distract from unpleasant experiences. These babies may be hard to soothe or put to sleep no matter what you try. About 10% of babies fall into this category. Babies who are fearful or slow to warm fall somewhere in the middle. They have difficulty adapting to or exploring new situations initially, but they are able to adjust over time. They tend to be less active and more mellow than other babies. These babies may initially struggle to adapt in certain situations but, as they get used to their routine, they become easier to care for. Around 15% of babies best fit into this category. If you're doing the math, you'll notice those numbers don't add up. During their research, Thomas & Chess found that the remaining 35% of babies didn't fit neatly into any one specific category, but rather displayed traits of all the categories at different times.

Thomas & Chess identified nine traits that helped determine what type of temperament a child has. These included the following:

- Activity level: amount of body movement and activity observed on a daily basis. Those with a difficult temperament typically have a higher level of activity (the need to move around, fidget, etc.)

- Biological Regularity: how regular a child's sleep/wake cycles, hunger levels, and bowel movements are. Difficult-tempered children tend to have a need for a strict, consistent, or rigid schedule (this can be in terms of when you eat, sleep, or what you do during the day)

- Adaptability: how quickly or slowly a child adapts to a change in routine or overcomes an initial negative response to an experience. Those with a difficult temperament tend to have more difficulty being open to or exploring new situations.

- Approach/Withdrawal: how quickly or slowly a child reacts and adapts to a new person or to an unfamiliar situation. Difficult-tempered children tend to struggle with adapting to unfamiliar situations.

- Sensitivity Threshold: how sensitive a child is to potentially irritating sensory stimuli, such as noises, temperature, crowds of people, textures, and tastes. Those with difficult temperaments tend to be overreactive to sensory stimuli (taste, touch, sight, sound, smell).

- Intensity of Emotional Response: how strongly the child reacts to both positive and negative situations and overall intensity of emotional expression, both positive and negative. Children with a difficult temperament are more likely to have an exaggerated range of emotional reactions. They may be seen as being too sensitive or dramatic, or they may experience emotions and emotional responses that don't fit the situation.

- Distractibility: how easily distracted the child is by an unexpected event or circumstance. Those with a difficult temperament tend to have a harder time shifting their focus off unpleasant experiences and are prone toward fixating on what went wrong. Even in the event of an unexpected but pleasant circumstance, these children are more likely to experience anxiety or distress around not being able to adequately plan or prepare for things.

- Quality of mood: amount of cheerful/pleasant behavior or mood contrasted with fussy, irritable, or sad behavior or mood. Children who have a more difficult temperament are typically more persistently negative and irritable.

- Persistence/Attention Span: how long the child keeps at a difficult task/ activity without giving up. Children with a more difficult temperament tend to have a more limited attention span. They give up more easily and tend to get bored more easily as well.

If you discover that you have a difficult temperament, then you know that your tendency will be to react strongly in situations where you feel uncomfortable, inadequate, or overwhelmed. As a mother, you are probably going to feel this way a lot. While it isn't easy to change your temperament or personality, you can increase your awareness of how you typically react and purposefully do things to counteract those reactions. For example, if you know that you tend to get worked up and flustered when your child starts acting out, a simple way to counteract those reactions would be to take a few slow, deep breaths before attempting to tackle the situation. It is also perfectly reasonable to give yourself a "time-out" so you can remove yourself from the stress of the situation and clear your head.

It will also be important for you to note whether or not you and your child have the same temperament. If you discover that both of you have a difficult temperament, it's likely that your relationship will be more volatile than if either of you had an easy temperament. People with difficult temperaments react strongly to situations and circumstances, so you can imagine what it would be like to have a mother and child, both with a difficult temperament, arguing over something such as when the child has to go to bed or take a bath.

Even before your children are old enough to talk back, there will be many times when your temperaments will clash with one another. Children with a difficult temperament will be much more attuned and sensitive to the emotions of those around them. If you have a difficult temperament and are becoming frustrated with yourself for not being able to soothe your difficult baby, then chances are that this will escalate your baby's reactions, which in turn will escalate your reactions, etc. This is why it is so important to become more aware of how both you and your children tend to react. If you know ahead of time that an interaction will be difficult or frustrating for either you or your child, then you can better prepare yourself mentally for that interaction.

It also would be helpful to maintain relationships with people who have an easy temperament and can mediate if needed in certain situations. Don't be ashamed to call on a partner, sibling, parent, or good friend to help bring a sense of calmness to the situation at hand. This is especially important when you're simultaneously trying to stay in a good place in terms of recovery from your eating disorder. As mentioned in the previous chapter, self-care is crucial in the postpartum period, and sometimes this will mean you need to have some time away from your children to better meet both your own needs and their needs. You will be a much better mother to your children if you are able to keep yourself in a good place mentally and emotionally. Allow others to help you with your children and take time to do things that will help de-escalate your emotions. Warm bubble baths, massages, or lying in bed with a good book are all good examples of how to bring your energy level down, but find things that best suit your individual needs.

Most importantly, however, recognize that having a difficult temperament isn't always a negative thing. If you or any of your children do have a difficult temperament, then it means that you and they also are likely to be consistent, reliable, passionate, determined, motivated, empathic, sensitive to surroundings and the needs of others, and zealous for life. Taking time to reflect on all the positive aspects of your and their personality can often help to offset the negative connotations that come with a difficult temperament.

What This Means

Your newborn's temperament is not your fault! Your infant's personality and temperament are due largely in part to genes. There's a good chance that the way you and your partner were while growing up will be reflected in the way your children express themselves as well. If you were a difficult child and your partner was an easy child (or vice versa), then it is likely that some of your children will be difficult and some will be easy. The way you react and respond to your children will shape and define their personalities further; but if you are a new mother with an infant that is nearly impossible to soothe, then it can often feel as though you're doing everything wrong and causing your baby to react so strongly. During these times, it is especially important to remember that having a difficult newborn does not make you a bad mother. It *does* mean that you are probably going to have to work harder to meet your infant's needs, and this in turn may actually help make you a better mother.

How Your Eating Disorder Affects This

Most people who struggle with an eating disorder have a drive to do things perfectly. When you are unable to do so, you may feel inadequate and insecure, and over time this can lead to self-hatred. This perpetuates the eating disorder for a number of reasons. The eating disorder can be used as a form of self-punishment for not doing things right (i.e., not being able to soothe your children or make them happy), or it can be used to regain a sense of control when you don't have control over your children's emotions or reactions. If you have a difficult child, then it is going to be very important for you to be aware of how eating disordered thoughts might come into play to make a difficult situation even worse.

Reflections

As discussed earlier in this chapter, mothers of difficult or slow to warm infants are likely to feel more inadequate than those with easy infants, because the reality is it will require more time and energy to make your baby happy. The negative thoughts and feelings you have about your parenting abilities and about your baby are normal, AND it is important to communicate these things to your therapist so they can help you reframe them into more helpful and adaptive ways of thinking.

Take some time to write down the negative thoughts and feelings about your parenting ability and style that you have encountered while learning to navigate the balance between your infant's and your own temperament. Consider using a format of first writing down a negative thought you have about your parenting abilities, then writing down how that thought makes you feel. Here are some examples:

Negative thought: I have no idea what I'm doing and I'm going to mess up my kid.

How this thought makes me feel: Terrified, sad, discouraged, and hopeless.

———————————

Negative thought: I can't stand it when my baby keeps crying and I can't get her to stop. Why can't I understand what she wants? I wish she would just shut up!

How this thought makes me feel: Inadequate, frustrated, scared.

———————————

Negative thought: What if I never figure out how to make my baby happy and comfortable?

How this thought makes me feel: Overwhelmed, defeated, depressed

———————————

I encourage you to take your reflections to your therapist and share them. Please note that you can do this reflection even if you have an easy baby – negative thoughts and feelings about yourself and your parenting aren't magically nonexistent if your baby is easier to soothe. In fact, when an easy baby does become upset, it might feel even more stressful and overwhelming for you because you aren't used to having to deal with such strong emotions from your baby.

Application

Sometimes when you're trying to care for a difficult baby, it can feel like you're the only one going through this. Your therapist will obviously be a crucial support for you during this time, but it would also be helpful if you could find other sources of support. If you were part of a Lamaze class during your pregnancy, try to stay in touch with and get together with some of the other women from this group. Chances are, many of them will be going through similar things as you.

Another good source of support can come from joining a Mommy and Me group. While the basis of this group is primarily to help foster the attachment relationship you have with your baby, it can also be a primary source of support as you come together with and get to know the other mothers who are a part of the group. Sometimes, all you really need is to hear that another mother is going through similar struggles as your own. Even if neither of you have come up with a brilliant solution, the comfort you will feel from realizing you're not completely alone in the difficulties you face will be irreplaceable.

Narratives

Dahlia has a history of Bulimia and has experienced some slips in her recovery since delivering her baby boy 8 weeks ago. Dahlia has identified herself as having a difficult temperament, while her baby is relatively easy-going and flexible. Dahlia has found that when her baby doesn't respond to the degree she would expect him to, she tends to either get anxious or frustrated. For example, after feeding her baby, she oftentimes can't tell if he is satisfied or full, and this makes her anxious about whether she's feeding him enough. If her baby is a little fussy and doesn't settle down right away after Dahlia changes his diaper or rocks him, she finds herself getting frustrated.

Angel has struggled with cycles of binge eating and over-exercising to try and compensate for her food intake. Angel has a 12-week-old baby boy who has been very difficult and colicky. Angel's baby rarely sleeps for more than 1-2 hours at a time, and when he is awake, he generally is very fussy. Angel has had a difficult time with feeding her baby, as he often seems uninterested in breast feeding and struggles to latch. When he does eat, he frequently spits up. Angel recognizes that she has characteristics of having a difficult temperament. She is feeling very discouraged and often thinks to herself that she is a bad mother and that her baby must hate her. Angel sometimes gets so overwhelmed with her baby's constant fussing that she can't tolerate being in the same room as him. She will beg her partner to take care of the baby, then will put on headphones and fixate on running on her treadmill. Afterwards, she often struggles with feeling extremely guilty for "abandoning" her baby and will try to compensate by interacting more with him. This level of interaction is sometimes too intense for her baby, who responds by fussing or looking away from Angel. This further insinuates to Angel that her baby hates her and that she isn't a good mother.

Nikki has a history of restrictive eating that is limited to what she determines are whole and "healthy" foods. She has a 10-week-old baby with a slow-to-warm temperament. She has found that her baby thrives on routine and becomes fussy when that routine is disrupted. This is challenging for Nikki, because she also has a 4-year-old who is constantly disrupting the routine Nikki tries to set for her newborn. Nikki is finding herself growing increasingly irritable with her oldest child. Rather than working to help her newborn adjust to changes in routine, Nikki is finding herself increasing her rigidity around her own and her infant's schedule and eating habits.

Take some time to reflect and journal about your reactions to the narratives you just read. Whose story do you most resonate with? Who did you have the hardest time feeling empathy toward, and what do you think made it hard for you to empathize with them?

Chapter 4:
Infancy and the Development of Trust & Attachment

Chapter 4: Infancy and the Development of Trust & Attachment

Unfortunately, infants don't come with instruction manuals. Even if they did, each baby is so unique and different, even the most detailed manual would have difficulty explaining how to raise each one perfectly. Despite this, there are several theories that adequately describe the general developmental and psychological milestones that your children (and you!) will have to cross as they grow and mature. Knowing these theories can help alleviate some of the confusion you may face when you encounter challenging situations.

Infancy can be a scary time for new mothers, because this is when the reality sets in that you now have the full responsibility of another living being. This is a crucial time developmentally for babies, and knowing that can add even more stress to your situation. However, it doesn't have to be that way if you can grasp a few simple factors about this period.

One of the most important things that happens for babies during this time is the development of trust and attachment. Even as infants, babies can pick up on whether their environment is a safe place. Development of trust and attachment takes place primarily through the mother-child relationship because, as the mother, you are typically going to be the primary caregiver. This is usually true even if you work outside of the home and have someone else watch your child during the day, because the bond with your baby starts when you carry it in your womb for 9 months. Babies learn to trust the environment based not only on whether you provide for their basic needs, but also based on your mental and emotional state when you're around them.

Infants can tell when something isn't quite right because, before the age of about 15 months, babies don't have an awareness of being separate from you. Because of this, they will regularly reference your emotional state and adjust their emotional state to match yours. If you interact with them when you're upset or stressed, they will internalize those emotions and interpret their environment as not being safe. Instead, if you exude warmth and safety, your infants will become more willing to explore their environment and let you out of their sight without becoming anxious, because they know that you are consistent and predictable. This pattern of modeling your thoughts, feelings, and behaviors is present throughout childhood, although it manifests itself in different ways at different times.

Attachment Styles

John Bowlby and Mary Ainsworth were two psychologists who studied the development of attachment in babies and young children. Through their research, they identified four different attachment styles: secure, anxious-ambivalent, avoidant, and disorganized. The latter three styles are sometimes grouped together and labeled more generally as insecure attachment.

Babies who are securely attached will actively explore their environment and aren't afraid to wander away from you, because they know that they can always return to you for reassurance when they need it. When you leave them, securely attached babies will become upset about the separation and will actively seek out comfort and contact with you as soon as you return. In order to develop a secure attachment, babies need to feel safe, be seen (i.e., have their needs met when they communicate those needs), receive comfort and reassurance, feel valued (i.e., have caregivers that genuinely enjoy and delight in them), and feel supported to explore. As a parent, consistency and predictability are key components to helping your child develop a secure attachment.

Babies who are insecurely attached may react a couple of different ways depending on the context of the separation and the environment in which the insecurity originally developed. Babies who have an anxious-ambivalent attachment style will cling to you and be unwilling to explore their environment both when you are with them and when you separate yourself from them. They will become distressed when you leave them, but then act ambivalently when you return, oftentimes both seeking out your comfort and pushing you away when you try to give it to them. Babies who develop an anxious-ambivalent attachment style tend to have caregivers who are inconsistent—sometimes their caregivers are attuned and attentive, and sometimes they are preoccupied and dismissive. This tends to develop uncertainty and anxiety in babies, because they are never sure how their caregivers will respond to them. Anxious-ambivalent children are also more likely to have parents who seek out emotional or physical closeness to meet their own needs rather than the needs of their children. These parents might be seen as intrusive or over-protective because they are too focused on themselves and how their child makes them feel rather than being fully attuned to the needs of their child. At the far end of the spectrum, children who are physically or psychologically abused, as well as those who experience an early physical separation from their primary caregiver, are at a higher risk of developing an anxious-ambivalent attachment style.

Babies who are insecurely attached and take on more of an avoidance pattern tend to ignore their mothers most of the time. When you are around, it is likely that they will behave as though you are not there and, when you leave, they will show little distress. Upon your return, they will typically ignore you as well. Babies who develop an avoidant attachment style tend to have caregivers who are not very emotionally expressive. These parents may be more reserved or hands-off when their babies reach out for support, reassurance, or affection. Babies will naturally increase their attempts to connect with their caregivers initially, but this often results in their caregivers becoming overwhelmed and, therefore, more distant.

Parents of avoidantly-attached children tend to have difficulty tolerating any emotions their children express, even positive emotions. They may be critical of their children, telling them to "calm down" or "toughen up." This sends a message to these babies that it is not ok or safe to express their emotions or seek out support from others. This often leads to an internalization of emotions. Outwardly, this may appear to others as if these children are very well-behaved and have good self-regulation. Generally, well behaved children are praised a lot more than children who don't have good control over themselves, so an avoidant attachment style is often inadvertently perpetuated by other adult figures in a child's life, such as extended family members or teachers.

Babies who are labeled as having a disorganized pattern of attachment present with a combination of anxious-ambivalent and avoidant attachment styles. These babies are likely to be highly reactive, oftentimes displaying intense anger or rage. A disorganized attachment style is usually only seen in babies and children who have experienced significant trauma or abuse. These children typically learn to develop a fear response to their caregivers. Having what should be a source of safety and comfort become a source of fear evokes a lot of confusion and disorientation in these babies. Their caregivers tend to be highly inconsistent and contradictory in their interactions with their babies, which results in these babies never knowing what to expect, when their needs will be met, or even if their needs will be met at all. Babies innately strive to develop closeness and attachment to their caregivers, but this instinct is complicated by their fear of their caregiver and often results in them being resistant to interactions with their caregivers. This typically leads babies to grow up questioning themselves and developing a mistrust of their instincts.

The good news is that most babies (approximately 65%) develop a secure attachment with their primary caregiver. The better news is that you don't have to be "perfectly attuned" to your babies all the time for them to develop a secure attachment. In fact, most research shows that mothers who are perfectly attuned 33% of the time and who are trying hard to be attuned but miss it another 33% of the time typically have securely attached babies. That means that one-third of the time you can be completely distracted or emotionally unavailable to meet your child's needs and they will likely still be just fine. This is often referred to as "good enough" parenting. Perfect attunement means that you are able to read the nonverbal and emotional cues, interpret them accurately, and respond appropriately to the needs of your infant. A concerted effort at attunement means that you are making an attempt to read, understand, and interpret those cues but that you don't get it exactly right.

The reality is, you're going to mess up sometimes. You will get tired, frustrated, and angry at your baby. You will also have times when you are completely preoccupied, oblivious, or confused about what your baby is going through. There is no way for you to fulfill every need, predict and avoid every painful or harmful situation, and fix every problem. In fact, if you were able to do all these things, it would actually be detrimental for your children because they would never learn to self-soothe, deal with disappointment, or cope with hurt and pain.

It's also worth noting here that it is entirely possible for babies to develop secure attachments in some relationships and insecure attachments in others. For example, for babies who have one caregiver who is physically and emotionally attuned to them and another who is aloof, cold, and distant, it is not only possible but probable that they will develop a secure relationship with the first caregiver and an insecure relationship with the second caregiver. If you are reading this as a parent who is trying your best to attach to your child, but you have a partner who is unable or unwilling to do the same, you may be concerned about the impact this may have on your child. It's important to remember that babies are incredibly resilient and, while obviously it's not ideal for anyone to be insecurely attached, it is 100% possible to learn to securely attach to people and view the world as a safe place if you have even one person in your life who is able to provide the space and time to foster that attachment.

Trust vs. Mistrust

Erik Erikson was another psychologist who studied the development of trust and attachment. He identified 8 stages of psychosocial development, with each stage denoting a specific conflict that people experience. He theorized that people have to master the conflict at each stage to successfully progress to the next stage.

In Erikson's first stage of development, he identified the conflict between trust and mistrust. This stage begins at birth and lasts through the first 12 to 18 months of life. At this time in life, infants are entirely dependent on their parents for their survival. They rely on their parents for food, shelter, safety, health, and love. Like Bowlby, Erikson believed that infants who have caregivers that meet their needs consistently develop trust of others and learn to identify the world around them as a safe and consistent space. Infants who don't consistently get what they need develop a mistrust of others and a fear of the world around them because they learn that their environment is unpredictable and inconsistent.

Erikson identified affection, comfort, and food as the three main needs for babies in this stage of development. Affection teaches babies that when they communicate, which is typically done through crying at this age, their needs will be seen, heard, and met appropriately. Comfort helps them feel safe and secure, with primary sources of comfort being shown by keeping them warm, bathed, and fed. Erikson singled out food from the other basic needs as the most critical of those needs. Even as an infant, babies are able to recognize their hunger cues and communicate when they need food. When infants get fed when they are hungry, this helps them trust that their need for nourishment will be met.

How Trust and Attachment Styles "Show Up" In Adulthood

Trust and attachment continue to develop throughout our lives and, as we grow up, our view of ourselves and others becomes shaped by the significant relationships we have. As adults, our attachment style will be the most evident in our interactions with those to whom we are closest, typically partners and children. The way in which we develop trust and attachment tends to be relatively stable over time, however this is not always the case. It is possible for those of you who had an insecure attachment to your parents or caregivers in childhood to develop secure attachment relationships with partners and with your own children; however you probably know that getting to this place of security takes a lot of work to undo the damage incurred from past experiences, especially if you experienced abuse or neglect in childhood.

Adults who are securely attached are able to regulate their emotions in interactions with others yet are also able to open up to and trust others when they are feeling vulnerable. They are able to communicate their needs to others, and they are comfortable with closeness and interdependency. They seek out and provide emotional support to others. They tend to be strongly goal-oriented and have a clear sense of what they want to accomplish in life. They are comfortable being alone and using that time to explore and pursue personal goals. They are able to be introspective and can reflect on how they relate and act within relationships.

Adults who have a primarily anxious attachment style tend to think highly of others but struggle with their feelings about themselves, typically exhibiting low self-esteem. They need constant reassurance that they are loved, worthy, and good enough. They are likely to have an intense fear of abandonment, and this can cause them to be overly jealous or suspicious of their partners. Their anxiety can cause them to manifest as clingy, desperate, and overly preoccupied with their romantic partners. They are afraid of, and sometimes incapable of, being alone. They are highly dependent on others to meet their emotional needs.

Avoidantly attached adults may appear outwardly to be self-confident, successful, and independent. They are typically social and easy-going, and they may have a lot of social connections and relationships. However, these adults tend to be very "surface-level" in their interactions with others and very rarely let others get too close to them. They often avoid intimacy or long-term, committed relationships. These individuals are also very likely to have a hard time identifying their own emotions or recognizing cues their body is giving them when they may be injured or sick. They tend to be very disconnected with their own needs, both emotional and physical.

Adults with a disorganized attachment style are typically inconsistent in their interactions with others. They manifest a combination of anxious and avoidant behaviors, but there is typically no rhyme or reason as to when and why they may act more avoidant vs. more anxious. They desperately want to be loved and to belong, but they are simultaneously fearful of developing closeness, so they protect themselves by pushing others away. These adults are more likely to engage in behaviors that perpetuate a "self-fulfilling prophecy." They make themselves vulnerable and dependent on others, but they live in constant fear of rejection. This causes them to engage in behaviors to push others away, which is typically an attempt at self-preservation. When others respond to those behaviors and do leave, this confirms to them that people can't be trusted and that it is not safe to develop close relationships with others.

How Your Eating Disorder Can Affect Attachment

Research indicates that women who have struggled with an eating disorder tend to have an insecure attachment to their parents. This may have been part of the cause of your eating disorder, or it may have perpetuated the eating disorder once it developed. In any event, if you grew up with an insecure attachment, then it may make things more difficult for you when you raise your own children because you never had a good role model of how to be as a parent.

This doesn't mean that you're doomed to have insecurely-attached children; it just means that you'll have to be aware of how your own upbringing might affect the way in which you relate to them. Even if you feel as though you had a secure attachment relationship with your own mother, there are many other aspects of your eating disorder that might make it difficult for you to attach with your children. Depending on where you are in your recovery, there may be times when you are working through your eating disorder and are otherwise unable to be attuned to or available for your children in the way you'd like to be.

As mentioned in a previous chapter, you may begin to struggle with attaching to your baby even during your pregnancy. If you're in a place where you are struggling with your body image or with consuming the appropriate number of calories needed to sustain both yourself and your baby, gaining pregnancy weight may be especially challenging for you. This in turn may make it harder for you to bond with your baby, because essentially, they are the cause for your weight gain.

Another challenging aspect of attachment may come in the form of feeding your baby. As was just mentioned above, one of the foundational ways infants develop trust and attachment with their caregivers is by having their food needs met. If you're in a place of struggling with food after giving birth, breastfeeding your baby may carry a lot of mixed emotions for you. In order to give infants what they need in your breastmilk, you will need to both watch what you eat and make sure you are eating enough to keep your milk supply up. Being the primary supplier of your infant's nourishment can be an incredible way to bond with your baby, but it can also be extremely triggering. It should also be made very clear that if you choose not to or are unable to breastfeed, that does not mean your child is at a higher risk of developing an insecure attachment to you. Just the act of feeding babies when they are hungry fosters the development of trust. Mealtimes are typically a time when you can be closest to your baby and develop a deeper relationship, but if you are simultaneously struggling with the food aspect of this time together, it may make this bonding time very difficult for you.

What You Can Do

Babies are incredibly resilient, and so if you're sitting here thinking that your infant may have an insecure attachment to you, then it is not too late to change things. One of the simplest things you can do to counteract insecure attachment is to spend more time with your children. This doesn't just mean being around them physically, but when you are around them you should also be mentally and emotionally present with them.

Many times, this is easier if you're able to get out of your everyday routine and do something different to change the atmosphere. Some ideas include taking your child to the beach, a park, or a local library or museum. However, if you're working full-time or have other responsibilities around the house or in your community, you may have limited time with your children. In that case, spending time with them can be accomplished by having them around you as you do those other things. In infancy, baby carriers, wraps, or slings are a great thing to utilize. This allows you to keep babies physically close to you, but also keeps your hands free so you can do whatever it is you need to do. As they get older, allow your children to be with you and help you do things such as cleaning the house, cooking dinner, going grocery shopping, or running errands.

You may think that this will be boring for your children, especially if they are too young to really help with what you're doing. This is why mothers usually have their children do something else while they're working. However, attachment has been shown to crucially affect the development of children, and they can't attach to you very well if they aren't around you. Even if you're preoccupied with chores or work while they're around you, just being in your presence will help promote the attachment bond. If you take little moments to make eye contact, smile, hug, or sing to your child amid what you're doing, you're facilitating that bond.

One of the most important things you can do to facilitate the attachment bond with your child is to heal the areas where you may have had insecure attachment. This is often done through individual therapy, as therapy is a good place to increase your self-awareness and identify core beliefs that facilitate the way in which you perceive the world and behave in it. Family counseling may also be appropriate, depending on how available and willing you and your family members are to delve into family dynamics.

If you're reading this book, it's likely that you've already done some work on yourself, especially if you have ever received professional treatment. However, chances are good that even if you did start to explore your attachment style as part of your treatment process, you didn't fully resolve the wounds that were inflicted upon you because of insecure attachment. If you're still holding onto things in your relationship with your parents that were hurtful to you, then those things are going to impact the way in which you see your relationship with your children (and other important people in your life). To be clear, therapy isn't necessarily the only way to heal yourself from these past hurts, but having the opportunity to talk to someone who doesn't know you and can have a more unbiased view of your situation can be incredibly helpful.

Reflections

1. Looking back on your relationship with your parents, how would you describe what your own attachment style was like with them? What patterns of behavior or reactions do you have that give evidence of this?

2. What, if anything, do you want to do differently from your parents regarding your attachment relationship with your baby?

3. What are you most fearful of as you develop attachment with your infant?

4. What do you think is your baby's current attachment style? Is there anything you want to change or do differently to improve your baby's attachment?

Application

One of the simplest ways to develop a secure attachment relationship and to practice being attuned to your infants is to mimic the things that they do. This is sometimes referred to as mirroring because you are literally reflecting back whatever you see them doing. If they smile, you smile. If they roll their eyes, you roll yours too. You can even attempt to match your breathing to theirs. This will not only help you enter into your infant's psychological state, but for babies who are a little older, it will also help them to develop a sense of self and to feel like they are truly important because they are being "seen" by you. It's important to maintain eye contact with your baby during this time, but you may notice that your baby will look at you, then glance away, then look back again. This is normal and actually is one of the first ways that your baby learns to self-regulate. If you've never tried it before, looking deeply into somebody's eyes can be a very intense emotional experience. While people generally crave this experience at times, we can only handle so much at one time, especially as a baby. Glancing away allows babies to momentarily separate themselves from the intensity, regulate themselves, then reengage when they're ready.

Narratives

Hayley is the mother of a 9-month-old baby girl. This is her first birthed child, but she experienced 2 miscarriages within a 2-year period at 4 weeks and 10 weeks before her successful pregnancy. One of her miscarriages required a D & C, which was extremely difficult for Hayley emotionally. Hayley has a history of Anorexia, and her doctor told her that her first miscarriage at 4 weeks may have occurred in part because Hayley's body weight was very low and she wasn't eating enough to sustain another life. Since that time, Hayley became diligent about weight gain and keeping herself nourished so she could have a successful pregnancy. She was at a healthy weight and was consuming an adequate number of calories when she experienced her second miscarriage. Even though her doctor reassured Hayley that this miscarriage was in no way her fault, Hayley continues to struggle with the belief and guilt that she did something to cause the miscarriage.

Since the birth of her daughter, she has been extremely anxious about her baby's health and well-being. In the weeks leading up to her delivery, she googled all the possible things that could go wrong in her labor and delivery. Her birth experience ended up going very smoothly and her daughter was born healthy, but Hayley's relief around this did not last long. She soon began agonizing over the potential for something to go wrong and was terrified that her baby would get very sick or die. She was so protective of her daughter that she didn't allow anyone besides herself or her partner to hold her baby for 6 weeks, and even after that time she only allowed immediate family members to have any contact with her baby for the next 6 months. Hayley kept her daughter in a bassinet right next to her side of the bed and woke up multiple times a night with a panicked thought that she had stopped breathing. Her baby is now in a crib in Hayley's room and sleeps through the night most nights, but Hayley continues to wake up multiple times a night to check on her baby and make sure she is still breathing. There have been times when she awakens her baby because she is fearful that something is wrong with her or that she has stopped breathing.

As her baby has grown and become more mobile, Hayley's anxiety has gotten worse. Developmentally, her baby is on track and is beginning to actively crawl and explore her surroundings. Hayley's friends and family have called her a "helicopter parent" on more than one occasion, after observing Hayley frantically hovering around her baby anytime she wasn't in a stroller or playpen and could freely move around. Hayley is also very nervous during mealtimes, as her baby is starting to be able to eat more foods. Hayley constantly worries that her daughter will choke on something, and she agonizes over how small to cut foods to avoid choking. She also stresses out about the possibility of her baby having an allergic reaction to something, so she has been very hesitant about introducing new foods to her. Hayley sometimes spends several hours a day cooking and preparing food for her baby.

Katherine has a 6-month-old son. This is her third child, but her older two children are fully grown, so she has not had to take care of a baby in almost two decades. Katherine wants to connect with her baby, but her pregnancy was unplanned, and she is having a hard time experiencing the same emotions and interest she did with her older children. Katherine is a single parent and is well-established in her career, so she also only took 4 weeks off from work after her son was born, and for 2 of those weeks she was working from home almost at a full-time capacity. While she ensures her baby's basic needs are met, Katherine has relied heavily on swings and playpens so she can keep him safe and soothed while she does what she needs to do. She also has hired a nanny to take care of her son while she is at work, as well as some times when she is at home but has other things she needs to do.

Prior to Katherine's pregnancy, she had been very focused on her body and appearance. She was an athlete growing up and was always watching what she ate so she could keep herself at peak performance. Katherine easily lost her pregnancy weight after her first two children and kept her weight at what she considered an "acceptable" range since then. However, she is now 20 years older and after having her last baby, Katherine has struggled getting her body back to how it was before her pregnancy. She now spends a lot of time stuck in a preoccupation with losing weight. After work, she works out on some home gym equipment for 1-2 hours, and she spends another 1-2 hours preparing her meals. This leaves her with very little time to engage with her son, and she finds that even when she tries to spend time holding or feeding him, she is usually thinking about other things and not fully present with him.

Anna has a 7-month-old and a 3-year-old. She works full-time but was fortunate to be able to take 4 months off work to heal and bond with her baby. She has both her children in day-care part-time, and her mother, who is retired and lives close by, watches them when they aren't in daycare. Anna has a rewarding but demanding job, and she is tired when she gets home from work. She often struggles to engage with her kids, but she makes a concerted effort to give them each some undivided attention before she jumps into the evening routine of making dinner, bathing her children, and putting them to bed. On the weekends, Anna tries to go out and do something fun with her children for a few hours on Saturday. There are also times when her energy and resources are low, so they end up staying home and engaging in more screen time than Anna would like, but this allows her some alone time to recharge, which she knows is much needed.

Anna has been in recovery from severe Bulimia for 5 years. In her late 20s, she had a period of time in in-patient treatment, then completed a step-down program which culminated in being able to manage her eating disorder with weekly outpatient therapy sessions. Anna experienced a brief relapse of her eating disorder after her first child was a few months old, but through increasing her therapy sessions and relying more on her existing support systems, she was able to get place to a stable place in her recovery.

Since having her second child, Anna better knows the things that can trigger a relapse for her, so she has been very mindful of making space for herself and her own needs, even though that sometimes means she isn't able to do everything she'd like to for her children. Anna has had periods of guilt and doubt surrounding her parenting abilities, but she tries to reassure herself that by taking care of herself, she is better able to "show up" for her children and be fully present with them when she spends time with them.

Take some time to reflect and journal about your reactions to the narratives you just read. What do you predict would be the attachment styles developed for Hayley's, Katherine's, and Anna's babies?* What attachment style do you imagine Hayley, Katherine, and Anna may have had growing up? Do you find yourself feeling critical or judgmental toward any of these mothers? Do you find yourself feeling worried or fearful about your attachment with your own children?

* It's important to remember that none of these scenarios in isolation can create or predict a specific attachment style. It takes consistent and persistent patterns of behavior to instill a more pervasive attachment style in a child. Being a "good enough" mother does not require perfect attunement to your children at all times!

Chapter 5: Toddlerhood—Autonomy & Independence

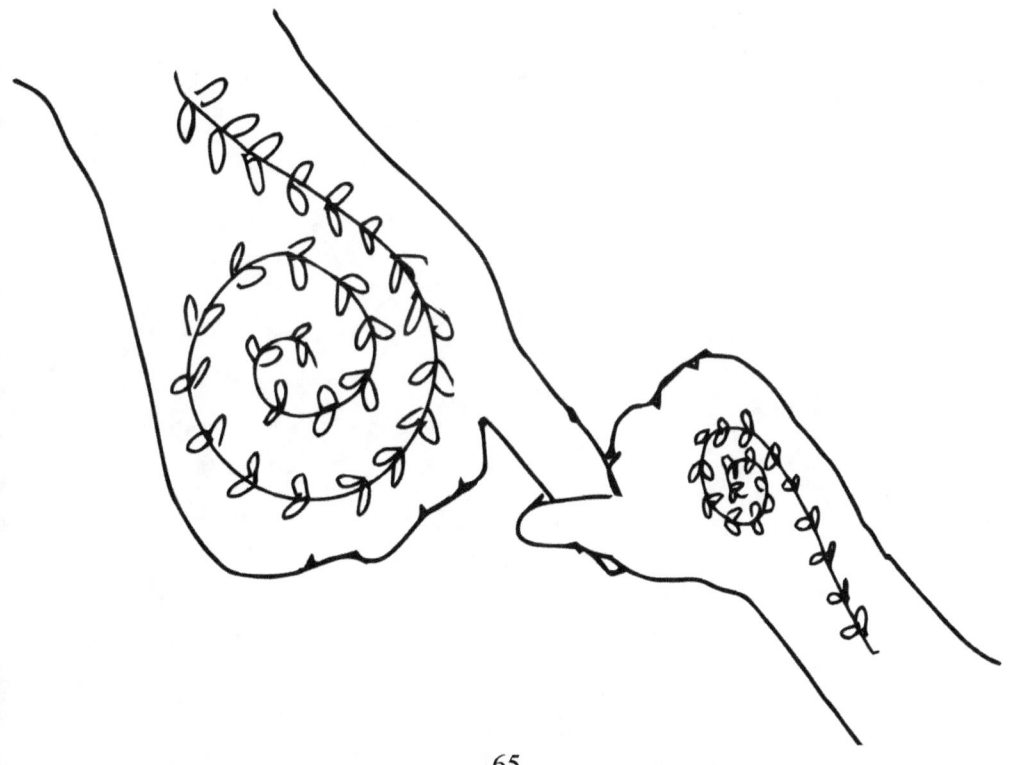

Chapter 5: Toddlerhood—Autonomy & Independence

The pull that babies have to separate from you is biologically and psychologically driven, and it is a necessary step in their development. When infants are first born, they have no concept that they are physically or emotionally separate from you. They slowly become more aware of their surroundings, but this initial alertness comes from their experience of still being completely connected to you. As far as they are concerned, they are one entity with you.

Starting at around the age of 9 months, babies naturally begin to venture away from the arms of their mothers and explore their individuality, although they still do not have an awareness of being separate from their mothers. Then, between the ages of 15-24 months, babies become increasingly aware of their separateness and now recognize you as your own entity: Mom. Initially, this can be distressing for babies, which is why there is often an increase in separation anxiety during this time. This means that anytime you attempt to physically leave, their level of anxiety rises and they become distressed at your absence. They usually react by clinging to you to stay close and reconnect with you in the way that was familiar to them when they perceived themselves as being one entity with you.

However, babies eventually learn to embrace this newfound separateness. As they develop into toddlers, they typically grow increasingly assertive in their need for independence. Developmentally, they are learning to become more autonomous with their bodies and actions, and they mimic this independence in their environment too. This is the stage in life when your children will start to become resistant to the limits you set.

Because they're still very young, the parental relationship remains the most important and primary relationship for toddlers, and they are very dependent on your reactions to their developing autonomy. If you react with fear or restraint toward their emerging independence, then they will likely develop a sense of shame and doubt about their abilities and actions. This may translate into an inability or a refusal to try and change the environment around them. Instead, they will turn their shame and doubt inward and over-manipulate themselves, often obsessively, to compensate.

This is the stage in Erik Erikson's model where children will either develop autonomy or a sense of shame and doubt. The main question at this stage of development is whether they can do things for themselves or are reliant on others. Toilet training is the biggest milestone event that happens during this stage, but there will be an emphasis on personal choice in a lot of areas such as getting to decide what to eat and being allowed to pick out what to wear. Toddlers who are allowed the freedom to expand their independence will pass through this stage feeling confident and secure. This in turn will make them more likely to experience success and confidence during later tasks, such as learning social skills or growing in their academic abilities. Those who continue to be controlled or prevented from making their own choices will be more likely to develop a sense of inadequacy and self-doubt.

Some researchers have looked at how this separation-individuation process we go through as toddlers can affect us in adulthood. As humans, we are driven to be in relationships with one another, yet we are constantly trying to balance our simultaneous needs for separateness and closeness. The degree to which we are allowed to differentiate ourselves as children influences our level of differentiation as adults. If toddlers are allowed the space to develop their own thoughts, feelings, and values, then they grow to become better differentiated as adults. If, instead, they are forced to conform their ways of thinking to others, then they never learn to think for themselves. It is argued that this keeps children and adults alike stuck in a place of fusion with others, which results in a poor ability to function overall, because they are easily influenced by whatever emotional environment they happen to be in. It has also been shown that parents who have a poorer level of differentiation tend to project that same level of differentiation onto their children.

What This Means

This is one of the most important times to let your toddlers loose to explore and discover the environment that surrounds them. This can be harder than it seems, especially if your toddler is your only or first-born child. Many mothers tend to be "helicopter parents," constantly hovering around their children out of fear that they might get hurt or make a mistake in some way. Mothers who do this are usually doing so out of a deep sense of love and concern for their child, and there is absolutely nothing wrong with that. However, try to think about it from a developmental perspective. Biologically, your toddlers are programmed to begin asserting themselves in more autonomous ways during this time in their lives.

This is, in fact, the way in which they learn the most about their environment and the rules and regulations that surround it. This may mean that they need to fall down a few times before they learn not to run so fast. It may also mean that they cut or burn their finger on something sharp or hot to learn about being cautious around potentially dangerous objects and appliances. Of course, you would never intentionally allow your children to do something that would seriously injure them, but at the same time you don't want them to go through life with a complete unawareness of the fact that their actions have consequences.

The struggle for autonomy will also manifest itself in less dangerous ways. Consider toddlers who are attempting to put together a puzzle for the first time. A natural reaction is to jump in and show them how to solve it. When you do this, however, it impedes the chance for kids to figure it out on their own.

This may not be a cause for immediate concern, especially if you only catch yourself doing it occasionally; but if you make a habit of always doing things for your kids, then you're taking away their opportunity to learn.

The context in which this takes place makes a huge difference too. Children who are quietly playing with the puzzle, and who are quite content with the fact that they are not doing it right, may be better off just being left to their own devices to allow the opportunity to figure it out. For children who are noticeably distressed or frustrated by the fact that they can't figure the puzzle out, this would be a perfectly appropriate time to step in, calm them down, and take the opportunity to model a *portion* of how to complete the puzzle. Notice that even in this case, however, you want to avoid doing it all for your children, because that may communicate to them that they are incapable of such accomplishments or that they will always need assistance in completing those kinds of tasks.

How Your Eating Disorder May Affect the Development of Autonomy

Having children who are now in the developmental stage of separating from you is difficult for most parents, but for anyone who has struggled with an eating disorder or other mental health condition it can feel especially threatening and intimidating. You have likely struggled for control in most areas of your life, and developing an eating disorder may be one manifestation of that drive for control. When you have children in this developmental stage, you are constantly being reminded of how little control you have. Things you used to be able to handle easily with them are now a struggle as they fight against your once fool-proof routines and rules. While this is a normal response for children to have at this age, their resistance can feel like another blow to your ego, perpetuating negative thoughts and feelings about yourself.

If you are an eating disorder survivor, you will likely need to work on relaxing your grip on your children and allowing them to take control over some things. One of the most difficult things for you to relinquish control over may be what your children eat. Aside from things they are legitimately allergic or sensitive to, you should not be completely restricting them from any food, even ones you may consider unhealthy. Of course, it makes sense to monitor their sugar intake and to provide whole foods as often as possible. However, completely restricting children from candy, pizza, or other "unhealthy" foods makes it more likely that they will either eventually rebel against that restriction and then struggle with their own self-control over their consumption, or that they will become overly fearful and anxious about needing to "eat healthy." In both of these scenarios, you could be priming them for the development of their own pattern of disordered eating thoughts and behaviors.

This doesn't mean you have to freely let your children eat their fill of fast-food burgers and fries, and there are many legitimate health benefits to primarily eating whole-foods. However, even in most of the current popular eating lifestyles today, there is room for eating foods that don't fall into that particular diet, with many encouraging an 80-20 approach, where the diet of choice is followed 80% of the time, and 20% of the time foods outside of that diet are allowed. Many families who follow a particular eating lifestyle choose to keep processed foods or sweets out of their home but allow for exceptions when eating out, traveling, at someone's house, or at a party or other gathering.

What You Can Do

One of the best things you can do to prepare yourself for this stage in the development of your children is to be aware that this is probably going to be a challenging time for you. It may seem counterintuitive to think that acknowledging and accepting the difficulty of this period would be remotely helpful, but there is something about giving yourself permission to struggle that is incredibly freeing.

It may also be helpful for you to reflect on your own childhood and explore the ways in which your life was or was not controlled, either by others or by external factors. Having gone through a battle with an eating disorder or any other mental health condition, you are undoubtedly aware of the fact that control plays a central part both in the development and the perpetuation of that disorder. While there are many factors that work together to create any mental health disorder, it is likely that your childhood consisted of times when you were not able or allowed to be in control of your circumstances. This may have occurred because of external factors such as an unexpected death in the family, a natural disaster, a global pandemic, or some other unforeseen trauma. However, it is equally likely that your own parents were over-controlling and didn't allow you the freedom you deserved and required when you were going through this stage in your development. This over-control may have come from your parents' drive to protect you, or it may have been rooted in their own psychological issues. In any case, the end result was that you were robbed of the opportunity to autonomously learn, grow, and make your own mistakes.

This leaves you with an interesting dilemma. You can make the choice to follow in the footsteps of your parents and control your children's lives much in the same way that yours was controlled. This may seem like the easier choice for several reasons. For one, it allows you to continue a cycle that, although maybe not ideal, is familiar and safe. It may even represent a sense of love and caring to you. Secondly, it allows you to have the control that you were once lacking in your own life. Having that sense of control can be a very powerful feeling.

However, take a moment to step back from this scenario and reflect on how others' control over you negatively impacted your life. Wasn't one of the most relieving things about developing your eating disorder the realization that you had *finally* found something to control that your parents couldn't do anything about? As your eating disorder progressed, however, you then began to realize that it was controlling you rather than the other way around, and the cycle progressed as you continually made attempts to control a life that was out of control.

By exposing your children to the same constraints that you were subject to when you were growing up, you will be creating that same sense of suffocation and drive to control something in their own lives that you experienced. While there are too many confounding variables to say for certain that your decision to control your children will result in them developing an eating disorder, you know from experience that when someone has control taken away from them, it often drives them to gain it in unhealthy ways. However, you have the unique opportunity to change the future of your children and break the cycle of maladaptive patterns of behavior. Even more amazing is that you can accomplish this simply by being aware of your children's need for independence and autonomy at this stage in their lives and making the conscious choice to relinquish your drive to control them.

Reflections

1. Reflect on some of the things that you had previously controlled in your toddler's life when they were younger that they are now taking autonomy over and list them below. Are there some things that are harder for you to relinquish than others? If so, what are your thoughts on why those particular things are more difficult for you? What steps can you take to help yourself let go of these things and allow your child the opportunity to develop their autonomy and independence?

2. Take yourself back to when you were the age of your toddler. If you can't remember that far back, then go back as far as you can. Think about the things in your life that your parents controlled and write them down. Also write down the thoughts and feelings you experienced from this. Many of these things might have been appropriate and, if so, then you may have felt a sense of safety and security. However, you may have perceived some of these things to have been handled in unnecessary or inappropriate ways. Feelings that may have been evoked from these experiences could include restlessness, frustration, anger, etc.

Application

It's one thing to talk about giving your child more autonomy, but to actually do it can be extremely difficult and even scary at times. As mentioned previously, one of the hardest areas to relinquish autonomy in as an eating disorder survivor is around food. One way to practice increasing your comfortability around this is to try to offer your children choices as much as possible. This doesn't mean you have to offer a "healthy" choice and an "unhealthy" choice, but rather that you allow for choices within reason that fit into whatever the meal is being offered or prepared. For example, you could give your children the choice between carrots or cucumber, chicken or salmon, rice or potatoes. You can let them choose their cup, utensils, and place settings. Depending on other factors and dynamics, you may even let them choose where they eat their meals, such as outside on the patio or as a picnic on the floor.

Finding an activity where you can practice the skill of relinquishing control can also be very helpful. One of the best ways to do this with toddles is to engage them in play that requires some type of emerging skill. This play could utilize something like a puzzle, a shape sorter, or a pegboard. It should be something that you know they do not have mastery over yet, because your challenge will be to let them figure it out without jumping in and doing it for them. However, it should also be something they have some familiarity with. Anytime a novel toy is presented, it absolutely makes sense to first demonstrate its use and purpose but, in this case, make it a familiar toy so that you can practice appropriately letting them be in control.

Stay engaged with your children and provide encouragement and reflection. If you see them doing something wrong or struggling in any way with the toy, then your first step should be to assess how they are feeling about it. If they are playing happily and seem perfectly content to keep trying, then there is absolutely no need for you to do anything. Trying to help your children in this scenario would be much more about managing your own anxiety than trying to manage theirs. If they have no anxiety about it, then let them be!

For children who are reacting in frustration or anger about their inability to get a puzzle piece in the right spot or something along those lines, then your initial intervention should still be a hands-off approach. Provide verbal encouragement to let them know that you see them struggling, yet that you believe in their ability to do it. The only time that you should directly intervene is if it becomes obvious that your child lacks the ability to do the thing they're trying to do, AND they're becoming frustrated or angry to the point where they're going to have a meltdown and not be able to continue the activity unless they get some help. Even in this scenario, however, it would be beneficial to have them try it again independently after you've helped them. This will encourage and promote autonomy and competency in them without shaming them for their inability to do something.

Narratives

Kelsey's son is 18 months old and fiercely independent. Up until this point, Kelsey has felt like she's been able to manage her own drive to control things, but just this week her baby has suddenly refused to breastfeed and will no longer let her help cut or prepare food once it is on his plate. If Kelsey touches anything on his plate, he refuses to eat it. He previously had been a good eater, but he has now become extremely picky and will no longer eat some of the foods Kelsey could bank on him eating, such as olives and bananas.

This drastic and sudden change in behavior is initially confusing and frustrating for Kelsey and, at first, she fights it by trying to assert control. She continues to give her toddler olives and bananas and continues to try and cut his food once it's on his plate. She believes she is doing the right thing and that this is a battle of wills that she must win.

As this continues, however, Kelsey's anxiety begins to rise, and she finds herself starting to crave control over her own eating habits again. As a teenager, Kelsey spent several years engaging in rigid rituals around food. She knows that her re-emerging disordered eating thoughts are a sign that she needs to make some changes.

Kelsey also starts to have more detailed memories around her own young childhood and how her own mother was very controlling over what Kelsey ate, forcing her to follow a vegan diet for several years. Kelsey recalls how this intense control over her food choices was a precipitating factor in the development of her eating disorder, and she knows she doesn't want to create that same scenario for her own child. She decides to try and allow her toddler some flexibility and choice. She begins to let him choose between 2-3 options for snacks and side dishes at mealtime, and she also models on her own plate how to break apart or cut food into bite size pieces so her toddler can watch and learn this himself.

Aliyah has a 2 ½ year old daughter who is a daredevil. Her toddler has always been advanced in her gross motor skills, walking at 9 months and running by 12 months. She is also a frequent climber. Aliyah decided to buy a toddler bed for her daughter shortly after she turned 2 because she learned how to climb over the railings of her crib, injuring herself once after falling. Since getting her new bed, however, Aliyah's toddler has been getting out of bed in the middle of the night and wandering around the house looking for things to play with. When out in public, if Aliyah doesn't watch her daughter like a hawk, she will almost always be found climbing or getting into something. Last week, they had a very close call when they were in a parking lot and her toddler ran right in front of a car that was backing up, however the driver fortunately saw her in time to stop.

Aliyah knows she needs to do something to better handle her toddler before something more serious happens, but she is struggling with how to do that. Aliyah's own upbringing was very strict and, as a teenager, she rebelled strongly against that, getting into drugs and alcohol and ditching school regularly. Aliyah developed Bulimia when she moved out of her parents' home, and she struggled for years with learning how to manage her food intake and stop binge eating. Her childhood had been so controlled that she never learned to regulate herself, and teaching herself how to control herself as an adult was very challenging. Aliyah has become so fearful of overcontrolling her child that she hasn't disciplined her much at all, and she is now in a situation where she doesn't know how to start setting boundaries and limitations for her daughter.

Take some time to reflect and journal about your reactions to the narratives you just read. What parts of each narrative do you most resonate with? Do you find yourself feeling critical or judgmental toward either mother? If so, reflect on what it is that triggers that feeling for you.

Chapter 6:
Early & Middle Childhood— the Time for Modeling, Initiative & Industry

*Chapter 6: Early & Middle Childhood—
the Time for Modeling, Initiative, & Industry*

Social Learning & Modeling

As perhaps is already evident, children derive a lot of their internal and external emotions and behaviors from what they observe in their parents. Some terms for this phenomenon include "social referencing" and "modeling". Babies and young children generally only have their parents to model themselves after, which is why the way you behave around your young children is so impactful. Children learn primarily through direct observation of others, and they are quick to absorb and copy the ways you think, feel, and behave.

Evidence of this has been shown in research over the years, with many studies confirming that babies use familiar adults' facial expressions to form their own judgments about unfamiliar people or situations. If they see their parent smiling at someone or in an unfamiliar situation, then they're likely to determine that person or situation is safe. If instead they see their parent frowning or looking upset, then they are more likely to judge that person or situation as being unsafe. Research has also shown how babies utilize social referencing as they age. About 50% of 14-month-old babies will refrain from touching a toy when their mother forbids them to touch it, and by the age of 22 months, almost 100% of babies will follow their mother's instruction. This shows how impressionable kids are to those in authority.

The concept of modeling goes beyond just following directions or assessing a situation as safe or unsafe. It also involves the way in which even babies learn to copy the actions of others. Researchers have watched as young children sat in a room with two adults who were engaged in play with a series of toys and activities. After the children watched the adults, they were left alone with the same toys and activities. The researchers found that the children were quick to model the actions and behaviors that they had just seen in both adults, however they were more likely to imitate the actions and behaviors of the adult who they perceived to be in charge of the interactions. This shows that children not only take in the words that they hear and act accordingly, but they are also able to discern authority and choose to imitate the behaviors of those whom they perceive to be in charge.

Of course, an interaction between any two individuals is a two-way street. Interactions consist of behavior, personal factors, and environmental factors; and all three of these interact interdependently. Children generally choose models who have similar characteristics to themselves, as well as those who exert the most power or influence over them. It makes sense, then, why little girls more often model after their mothers while little boys tend to model after their fathers.

If parents have so much influence and impact on their children, then you may be wondering why children raised in the same household can sometimes turn out so differently. This is because the process of modeling in children is actually pretty complicated. Albert Bandura was a psychologist who created Social Learning Theory. He built on previous theories that emphasized behaviorism (such as Pavlov's classical conditioning theory and Skinner's operant conditioning theory) and shifted the focus onto how social factors play a crucial role in learning and behavior. He proposed that observational learning especially was key, so much so that he believed children were more likely to repeat something they had merely observed than they were to repeat something they had directly participated in.

Bandura theorized that for a modeled event to be internalized and learned, children have to go through four steps. First, they must have been paying attention and have correctly perceived the most crucial parts of the modeled event. Secondly, they must remember, not just notice, the behavior that occurred. Remembering comes from placing information into a symbolic image in their mind so that they can bring it to remembrance even when the model is no longer present. Thirdly, they need to figure out how to convert that image into action – in other words, they learn how to mimic what they have seen. If they are physically or otherwise incapable of repeating that behavior, modeling won't occur. Finally, they must have some incentive or motivation to act out the modeled behavior they observed. All behaviors have consequences, and if those consequences are perceived as rewarding vs. punishing, or if the positive outweighs the negative, it is more likely to be imitated.

If any of these four steps is missing, then the modeled event won't be retained. Bandura's hypothesis that more learning occurs through observing an event than is learned by experiencing it directly was based on the belief that observing an event allows more space for these four steps to occur. When you're experiencing something directly, you often need to make quick decisions or go through a trial-and-error process; but when you observe an event, you get to live vicariously through someone without being put under the same level of pressure. This allows more space for your brain to encode and process what is going on.

However, even vicariously learned events may not always stick. This is where all the individual factors of each person enter in. Things like temperament, personality, and prior experiences all affect whether or not you retain an event. Knowing this, it makes sense why one of your children may copy your every move while another one hardly seems to notice anything you do.

Psychosocial Development

The third stage of Erikson's psychosocial development model occurs in the preschool years (ages 3-5) and deals with the contrast between developing initiative vs. guilt. In this stage, children are starting to become more independent. They are learning to assert control over things and are discovering where they have power and authority and where they don't. It is at this stage that children begin to engage in more social interactions, typically because they are now in preschool and around peers more often. However, these skills are still largely fostered through the parent-child relationship as well. It is during this age that kids are learning to direct play and other social interactions, and they are developing skills as both leader and follower. Children who are successful in this stage go on to develop confidence and feel capable of leading others. Children who struggle with this stage tend to develop self-doubt. They may question or feel guilty about their drive to be in control of things, and they may also struggle to develop an initiative to accomplish things or set goals. During this time, children also first identify the concept of good vs. bad and start to find evidence to determine whether they themselves are good or bad. They are striving to find a sense of purpose, which in turn helps drive ambition and direction.

Erikson's fourth stage is industry vs. inferiority and takes place during middle childhood (ages 6-11). In this stage of development, children are learning to develop a sense of pride for their accomplishments and abilities. Those who receive encouragement from authority figures tend to develop a sense of competence, whereas those who do not have a source of encouragement frequently feel inadequate or inferior, and they are less likely to accomplish or even set goals. Peers also play a vital role during this stage of development, as children are beginning to learn to compare themselves to others. The concept of good vs. bad starts to solidify, and children are more frequently trying to determine what they need to do to be "good." This is the stage when self-confidence (or lack thereof) develops, and how children feel about themselves is largely rooted in the way others interact with them.

What This Means

The early and middle childhood years are complex in terms of development, and the influence of others is a large part of how children learn to identify how and where they fit in compared to others. Even if it doesn't always seem like they're paying attention, your children watch what you say and do, and they are quick to pick up on ways to talk and behave. As the parent, you are the first and most influential model your children will have. This does not mean that you need to hyper-focus on every little thing you say or do when they're around you. At the same time, however, it is important that you realize how much of an impact you have on your children. Little comments that you make about yourself, your children, or other people are quickly internalized into the way your children perceive themselves and others.

How others respond to them largely determines whether children grow up feeling confident or incompetent. If you, as a parent, create an atmosphere where you allow your children to make mistakes and learn from them, this helps instill them with the feeling that they have control and power over themselves. If, instead, you structure their environment so they don't have the means or ability to do anything wrong or mess up, or if you create a rigid environment where everything is criticized, your children will be more likely to grow up feeling incompetent and disempowered, and this will also affect their drive and motivation.

How Your Eating Disorder Affects Social Learning & Modeling

Low self-esteem and feelings of inferiority or incompetence are common among those who have struggled with an eating disorder, and these things are often perpetuated by critical thoughts and feelings about yourself. These negative thoughts and feelings can seep into the things you say about yourself around others. You may not even be aware that you're talking about yourself so critically, because those thoughts have often become a part of your constant internal dialogue. You're more likely to speak freely and not think much of it if you're in a comfortable setting, such as around your children and family. This is a natural occurrence; however, it is important to remember that, especially in early and middle childhood, your children are like sponges. They soak in everything they see and hear, then eventually "squeeze" it back out.

Being caught up in your eating disorder may make you less aware of how you are presenting yourself to your children, something that can be particularly crucial because they are watching your every move. When you're feeling unhappy or disappointed in yourself, this is likely to be reflected in your affect, your words, and most importantly in your actions. You may be more prone toward making negative comments about yourself, your appearance, your parenting abilities, or several other things. You may also turn your frustration toward other people, including your children, leading you to make negative comments about them and their abilities.

When your children hear you talking badly about yourself, they are more likely to turn around and speak poorly about themselves as well. This makes a lot of sense if you think about it. You are a trusted, knowledgeable figure in their lives. You are also related to them, which means that they are like you. If you communicate to them that there is something "wrong" with you, then it follows that they would think there is probably something wrong with them too. If they hear you calling yourself fat or ugly or stupid, then chances are good that they're going to assume that they are those things too. Conversely, if they hear you saying positive things about yourself, then they'll be more likely to think positively about themselves as well.

It is likely (though not a certainty) that the development of your eating disorder and comorbid struggles you've had came from growing up in an environment that caused you to feel incompetent and inferior to others. As an adult, this can manifest in many ways, but it is common to develop a drive to always be in control of things, as well as to become overly judgmental or critical of others. You may be more rigid and tend to see things as black and white. All these things can and will affect the way you interact with and relate to your child. You will need to be very mindful of how you navigate through times when your child makes a mistake, does something incorrectly, or falls short of an ideal you may have had in your mind.

What You Can Do

Depending on where you are in your recovery, your self-talk and your tendency to criticize or judge others may be difficult for you to monitor and change in the moment. However, keep in mind that you don't have to be completely free of these negative thoughts and feelings to change what you voice out loud when you're in front of your children. It's entirely possible that you could be thinking negative thoughts in your head yet make a conscious choice to either speak something positively or not voice anything at all.

Your children may be perceptive, but they don't have access to your inner thoughts. The more you're able to filter yourself, the less negativity your children will be exposed to, and the less likely they'll be to speak negatively about themselves or others. Any interaction you have with your children has the ability to create positivity in them, just as much as it has the ability to create negativity. Even when you're going through your own personal struggles, there are techniques you can learn to help ensure that the only thing your children sense from you is love and acceptance.

One excellent model for learning how to relate to your child positively and effectively comes from a type of intervention called Parent-Child Interaction Therapy (PCIT), developed by Dr. Sheila Eyberg. There are many components to PCIT, and if you are interested in learning more, I'd encourage you to do some research on it. However, for the purposes of this book, I will be highlighting the 5 basic skills utilized within this therapeutic model, as they can be used to enhance your ability to be a positive role model for your children. These skills are meant to be utilized during what is called, "Special Playtime," meaning it is a designated time that is intentionally set aside for you and your child to play together. These 5 skills include praise, reflection, imitation, description, and enthusiasm.

Praise can take two different forms — labeled and unlabeled. Unlabeled praises show admiration without saying specifically what it is that you like. This could be something like, "Good job!" Labeled praises allow you to be specific about the things your children do that you like, such as "Good job counting those blocks!" Both types of praise are useful, but labeled praises help your children learn exactly what they can say or do to receive more praise in the future. All children crave praise, so if they know exactly how to get it, then this ultimately will be more helpful for them. Labeled praise can be used proactively to increase positive behavior and improve self-esteem. Remember, your children believe whatever you say, and whatever is modeled for them is what becomes internalized.

Reflection is simply repeating the essential idea of what your children say. You are free to expand or use subtle correction in your reflection, so long as you don't alter the basic point they were trying to get across. For example, if your child says, "I doed it myself!" you could reflect something like, "You did it all by yourself!" If your child says, "Me mad," after someone takes their toy, you could say, "You're angry that Billy took that toy from you without asking."
Imitation means that you engage with your children in whatever activity they're doing and try to do it in a similar way. This communicates to your children that you are paying attention to them and that you're interested in what they're doing. This will also help you to stay engaged with them at their

developmental level, and it provides an avenue for them to feel like they have mastery over something and can be the teacher. One of the coolest things for a kid is to have an adult say, "Can you teach me how to do that?"

Description is a way for you to observe and point out whatever it is that your children are doing. Descriptions should be behavioral and directed toward your child, meaning that you use the word, "You" as you describe what your children are doing, such as, "You're coloring that circle blue." Descriptions assure your children that they have your undivided attention, and it also allows them to continue setting the pace for the activity. Descriptions are not meant to include any sort of opinion, even a positive opinion. This means it is not a time for you to provide your opinion about how well they're coloring or whether you think it's a good idea for them to color the circle blue.

Enthusiasm simply means that, in all your interactions with your children, you should do your best to maintain a lively voice that reflects your interest in what your children are doing. Being warm and engaged with your children will help boost their self-esteem and will foster the attachment relationship between you. There will undoubtedly be things that your children want you to do with them that are not even remotely enjoyable for you. For example, when your kid wants you to read the same book for the one hundredth time or watch the same movie or tv show on repeat, it's understandable that those things may not bring joy to your heart. This is one of the few times where I would venture to say it's ok to lie to your kids. It's ok to act thrilled to read the same book even if internally you want to scream. The point is that your children should feel like you genuinely want to spend time with them regardless of what you are doing together.

Sometimes the things you don't do are just as important as the things you do. In Parent-Child Interaction Therapy, there are certain things to avoid doing while you're engaging with your children. These include commands, questions, criticism, and sarcasm.

Commands take the reins away from your children and can set them up for failure if they disobey those commands. Giving a command when your children are in a dangerous situation or when you are setting a limit with them is one thing, but we can easily fall into the habit of giving commands for noncritical things as well, such as during play. Whenever you are engaged in Special Playtime with your children, you should not be commanding them to do anything unless they are doing something that is dangerous or could hurt themselves or another person. It doesn't matter if they are doing it "wrong" or playing with something in an odd or unusual way. This is not the time for teaching, it is the time for engaging.

Avoiding questions is tricky, because we are typically socialized to ask a lot of questions of our children. However, questions are another way in which you may inadvertently take the lead away from your children because it causes you to direct the conversation instead of just following it. Asking questions can also put children on the spot and make them feel like they must perform for you by responding in a certain way. Questions can bombard and overwhelm children, and ultimately, they can have the opposite effect of what you want—rather than getting them to talk to you, incessant questions can actually make them shut down and decrease their level of responsiveness toward you.

Criticism and sarcasm are to be avoided for several obvious reasons. They really don't help decrease problem behaviors, and in fact they can increase them at times. I mentioned before that children strive for attention, and if they don't receive it in the form of positive praise and attunement, they will seek it out in negative interactions with you. Words to avoid that will help you stay away from sarcasm and criticism are "no," "don't," "stop," "quit," and "not."

These words aren't helpful because they are only telling your child what not to do, rather than what they should do in its place. All the words on the "avoid" list dampen your child's self-efficacy, and they put a negative filter on your interactions with each other.

One thing to note: PCIT is typically implemented within the context of family therapy interventions and is guided by a therapist who has been trained in the PCIT model. You have been provided with some highlights of this model to assist you in your interactions with your children. However, if you find yourself struggling with engaging positively with you child, it would be recommended that you look into working with a PCIT specialist.

Reflections

1. Your chances of being able to filter your inner thoughts and feelings about yourself when you're around your children will be greater if you also have times and places where you can safely vent about how you're really thinking and feeling. One such safe space to do this is with your therapist. If you catch yourself having negative thoughts and feelings about yourself during the week, then take the time to write them down rather than voicing them out loud. This both gives you permission to have the thought, and it symbolically allows you to release that thought by pulling it out of your brain and putting it on paper. Then, when you are with your therapist, you can go through what you wrote down and talk about things as needed.

2. Now that you know how much the thoughts, feelings, and behaviors of children are impacted by what they see and hear from their parents, trace your own internal experiences back to their origin. What things do you remember hearing your parents say about themselves that had a lasting impression on the way you perceived yourself? What do you remember them saying about you that left a lasting impression on how you thought

and felt about yourself? The ability to identify the root of your own negative thoughts and feelings will help you be more conscious of what you are perpetuating in your own children.

3. Reflect on Erikson's stages of psychosocial development and how that played out in your own childhood. Did you successfully navigate the stages of initiative vs. guilt and industry vs. inferiority? If so, what contributed most to that? If not, what were the biggest barriers that got in your way?

4. Take a look at the PCIT descriptions of what to do and what to avoid in your interactions with your children. What things are you already doing with your children that come easily to you? What things do you foresee being the most challenging for you to incorporate into play with your children? Do you have any memories of your own parents playing with you? If so, how often did they utilize the skills discussed?

Application

One way to filter the negative thoughts and feelings you have about yourself is to reframe them in a neutral or positive way before voicing them out loud. It's not even required that you believe the created reframe, only that you voice it and, more importantly, that your children hear you voice it. Some people find it helpful to practice positive self-statements in front of a mirror. Others prefer to recite them internally, almost like a meditation, before verbalizing them. Find something that works for you and go with it.

If, while doing this, you find it too difficult to come up with something positive to say about yourself, focus instead on something positive to say about your child. This will still serve the purpose of ensuring you verbalize only positive things in front of your child, and it will also function as an esteem-booster for your children. Better yet, voicing the positive may even help pull you out of whatever negativity you were in previously.

One of the best ways to acquire the skills talked about in the PCIT section is to set up specific times to practice them (Special Playtime). Special Playtime should be done very intentionally during the times when you're engaging with your children. Allow your children to pick out a few preferred toys and engage with them in play, remembering to follow their lead and allow them to direct the play (so long as they are being safe with it). The toys do, however, need to be interactive and something you can easily join in with them. Video games won't work well for this because the level of interaction required is not that high. However, things like playdoh, puzzles, dollhouses, racecar tracks, etc. would all be appropriate choices. For more specialized instruction and direction, consider looking into doing PCIT sessions with a licensed therapist.

Narratives

Susan has struggled with her body image since giving birth to her daughter 4 years ago. She used to be a competitive athlete and has always been very conscious of both what she puts into her body and how her body looks. Susan has struggled with compulsive exercise and fasting to keep her weight down. She hasn't done either of those things since becoming pregnant with her daughter, and she is no longer competing in any sports, however this has been causing her to struggle with her identity. She is not in the shape she used to be in, and she tends to fixate on that. Susan frequently stands in front of the full-length mirror in her bedroom and squeezes her skin around her stomach. She doesn't usually say anything out loud, but she will frown and sigh, and internally she tells herself how disgusting her stomach is and how she is "letting herself go."

One day Susan finds her daughter in her bedroom, squeezing her stomach and frowning and sighing. Susan asks her what she is doing, and her daughter asks, "Mommy, am I fat?" Susan is taken aback and says, "Of course not, honey, why would you think that?" Her daughter turns around and faces Susan, then she states, "Well, don't you think you're fat? Isn't that why you look so sad when you look at yourself?" Susan found out her daughter had been looking into her bedroom and watching Susan whenever she was in there.

Hannah works full-time and has a very demanding job. She is a single mom and is exhausted when she gets home. She struggles to find the energy to play with her 3-year-old son, and when she does, she typically finds this to be very stressful. Hannah is very organized and structured, and having a child has been hard for her because of how much it disrupts her routine.

Hannah exerts more control over her son than she needs to, even during play. She becomes agitated when her son struggles to color inside the lines, and if he colors something the "wrong" color, she immediately corrects him. Hannah is beginning to worry that her son is advanced enough to succeed in preschool, so often instead of engaging with him in play she spends time trying to get him to memorize the alphabet and to learn to count. Hannah grew up in a high-achieving family where a lot was expected of her. She developed symptoms of Anorexia as a young teenager as a way to "master" her body, and she found that the control it gave her was very soothing, because she had finally found something that she alone could control and dictate.

Julie has struggled with being overweight for most of her life. She was often bullied as a child by her peers, and she struggled with her self-esteem as a teenager. Her parents were highly accomplished doctors and didn't seem to have much interest in Julie, especially compared to her older sister, who was very smart and accomplished like her parents. Julie utilized food as a source of comfort and to give her something to do, as she was often home alone without much to entertain her. She would often binge eat while watching tv. This made her feel even more inferior and incompetent, and she would get angry at herself for not having control over her eating habits.

Julie became pregnant at 16 after a boy she had a crush on finally seemed to notice her, but he quickly moved on after finding out she was pregnant. Julie's daughter is now 8 years old, and she also struggles with being overweight.

Julie works hard to make her daughter feel loved and worthy, because that was something she never received as a child. However, she also pressures her daughter to work hard and do well in school, because this was something she always struggled with. Julie's daughter is "smart" like Julie's older sister and parents, and she finds herself living vicariously through her daughter's accomplishments. Julie has unintentionally placed a lot of pressure on her daughter to succeed and have a better life than Julie did. Her daughter also struggles with her own self-esteem and finds it confusing how much Julie tries to build her up and encourage her when she is so critical and unmotivated toward herself.

Take some time to reflect and journal about your reactions to the narratives you just read. What narrative do you most identify with? Who do you feel most critical toward? How would you hypothesize these women navigated the psychosocial stages of initiative vs. guilt and industry vs. inferiority? How do you predict their children will navigate those stages?

Chapter 7: Ecological Systems

Chapter 7: Ecological Systems

The previous chapters have focused a lot on the parent-child relationship, but the truth is there is a lot more at play that influences us. We all constantly function within several different environments or "systems." These systems influence our thoughts, feelings, behaviors, and overall development. However, we are not just passive recipients of these systems. Who we are and how we behave within each system simultaneously influences the members of those systems. All people and environments with which we interact are a part of these systems, but how much influence they have over us can vary widely.

Urie Bronfenbrenner was a psychologist who developed Ecological Systems Theory. He was critical of other child development theories because he felt like they were too unidirectional, focusing too much on how the mother affects the child, rather than exploring how the child influences the mother or how they both influence and are influenced by the environment around them. He also viewed most other theories as not being ecologically valid, criticizing how research was done in a sterile laboratory and didn't reflect the complexities of the actual environment we live in. Bronfenbrenner's theory examines the various environments and systems we're a part of, and he broke these down into 5 main systems, each of which is nested within the others.

At the center of this "nest" is the core system, which is called the microsystem. For children, this consists of their immediate home environment and the people in it. Typically, this will include their parents, siblings, and other close family members such as grandparents or aunts and uncles. As children get older, other environments can become microsystems as well. This might include their school, church, or sports team, as well as all the people with whom they interact in those environments. Microsystems consist not only of the physical location or a specific event that took place within that system, but also the unique expectations and perceptions of each child as they function within that microsystem. Influence within the microsystem is considered to be bidirectional, meaning each person not only is influenced by the people and environments around them, but they simultaneously influence those people and environments.

The second system is referred to as the mesosystem. This system encompasses the connections between children's microsystems. Within the mesosystem, Bronfenbrenner emphasized that microsystems don't function independently but instead are interconnected and influence one another. This could include things like the way in which parents relate to their children's teacher, or how a child interacts with friends from school when they come over for a play date. Essentially, the mesosystem is a system of microsystems.

The third system is the exosystem. This includes environments in which the child isn't directly a part, but that still affect and are affected by the child. This might include things like a parent's job or a sibling's school. Mass media is also considered an exosystem. Any events or changes that take place in an exosystem can stir up changes in the microsystems as well. For example, parents who have a really bad day at work (exosystem) might come home (microsystem) and be more irritable with their children.

The fourth system is the macrosystem. This consists of all the standards, values, and influences that our society has on the micro-, meso-, and exosystems. It also includes the various cultural components that can influence development including socioeconomic status, race, ethnicity, the political climate, and religion. Rather than focusing on a child's specific environments, the macrosystem looks at the already established society and culture within which the child lives. The ways in which families, schools, and businesses function in one society can be very different from how they function in another society. For example, a child growing up in a poverty-stricken environment with few resources will grow up very differently and develop a very different worldview than a child growing up in a wealthy environment where there is an abundance of resources.

The fifth system is the chronosystem. This system contains all the environmental and historical changes that take place across a child's lifespan. These can include normal life transitions such as graduating high school or dating for the first time, as well as less common life transitions such as parents getting divorced or experiencing significant illness or injury. Historical events are also included in the chronosystem, such as the election of a new president, or something we've now all experienced, the emergence of a global pandemic.

What This Means

As important as the parent-child relationship is, it would be naïve to think that it will be the only thing to influence your children. As they grow up, your children will have a million different things that will influence them both positively and negatively. These will include peers, friends, teachers, sports and extracurricular activities, books, political and religious viewpoints, and social media. However, the research still holds that the influence parents have on their children remains primary.

This makes sense if you think about it using the metaphor of a tree. Many things can influence the growth and appearance of a tree. Sun and rain in moderation help to nurture it, while droughts, strong winds, and heavy snow can severely damage it. However, the thing that best determines the survival of that tree is the strength of its roots. Trees whose roots are firmly planted in rich, deep, nutrient-filled soil can withstand a great deal of extreme weather conditions. If, however, that tree is planted in shallow, rocky soil that is depleted in nutrients, even the smallest change in weather can weaken it or knock it over.

I envision parents as the soil that either fosters or inhibits the growth of their children's "roots." As the soil, you don't always have control over the various natural elements that come against your "trees," but you do have control over the most important thing—their foundation. The more you are able to provide a nurturing, safe atmosphere for your children to grow in, the more protective factors they will have when they are faced with "harsh weather conditions." Better yet, the more they will be able to discern between healthy environments and unhealthy ones.

How Your Eating Disorder Affects Ecological Systems

If you've struggled with an eating disorder, you know what it feels like to have tried planting your roots in shallow, dry soil. Part of the reason why your eating disorder progressed in the first place was probably because you didn't have a lot of protective factors surrounding you, which means that all of those external elements that work to hinder your growth came against you, and you didn't have a way to really protect yourself from them. When left to our own devices, we often tend to adapt in ways that seem to fix the problem in the moment but ultimately are destructive. An eating disorder is a way of trying to gain control and protect yourself from the harsh weather elements that come against you; but when you're grappling to keep your roots planted in rocky, shallow soil, this usually doesn't go very well.

Hopefully, by this point in your life, you have also had healing experiences and have developed relationships with people who have been a source of nurturing and protection. Being able to provide a nutrient-rich environment for your children as they grow is important to you, but it can be a big challenge whenever mental health issues or other circumstances are involved. It's hard to consistently give your children everything they need to mature and flourish in their development while simultaneously doing the same thing for yourself. This does not mean it will be impossible to give your children a strong foundation and, in fact, your drive to provide that for them may be even stronger given that you know what it feels like to not have had that protective factor for yourself. What it does mean is that you probably will need to work harder and overcome more barriers to ensure this firm foundation than are others who have not struggled with an eating disorder at any point in their lives.

What You Can Do

To some degree, you may be able to mediate some of the things your children are exposed to that could either stunt or enhance their growth. For example, you can control how much television your children watch and what types of shows they're exposed to. You can pick which school they attend, and whether or not they go to church or participate in extracurricular sports, clubs, or other activities.

Most importantly, you can control the type of atmosphere they're exposed to at home. This is important to keep in mind because there are millions of things within the different layers of systems that you won't be able to control. You can't always have power over things such as how your children are treated by peers at school, or what and when they learn about sex or drugs from friends or simply from their exposure to media influences. However, by mediating their home environment, you will be providing them with the tools and resources they need to make the right choices and behave in the ways you want them to when they are exposed to less-than-ideal circumstances.

Reflections

1. Thinking back on your own childhood, how would you describe your foundation, "root system," and subsequent growth experiences? What things contributed to making your soil richer and more nutrient-filled? Which things depleted it?

2. How do you envision your children's foundation being richer and more fertile than yours was when you were growing up? What things do you want to be different for them? What would you keep the same?

3. What is your biggest concern about some of the negative or adverse things your children might be exposed to as they develop new microsystems and begin to be influenced by things within the larger exo- and macrosystems?

Application

You'll be better able to manage your children's atmosphere and instill positive influences on them if you have a good grasp on the kinds of things they're exposed to on a daily basis. Make it a habit to check in with your kids when they get home from school or from any other out of home event or activity. Find out how their day went, what they did and talked about, who they were around, etc. This will provide you with the information you need to get a better idea of the positive and negative influences on your children, and subsequently will help you make informed decisions about what things need to be changed or talked about in greater detail. It will also provide the expectation that your children should always engage in open communication with you, which will be particularly helpful as your children grow up and their systemic influences expand. If your children are exposed to something that is potentially concerning to you, this will be an opportune time to instill in them your thoughts, feelings, and values. Even if you can't change the influences, you can attempt to change the way your children are affected by those influences.

Another way to monitor the things to which your children are exposed is to be an active participant in their daily activities. The first step to this is determining what kinds of things you want your children exposed to. Activities might include children's church, club soccer, dance classes, girl scouts, etc. But beyond just enrolling them in these activities, see how you can be involved in them too. Depending on your current work schedule, you could also do things such as volunteering in your child's classroom. By getting involved in things like this, you will have full access to the environments your child is in, and you will have more awareness of the things influencing your children.

Narratives

Krystal is an eating disorder survivor. Having battled bulimia and binge eating disorder for a decade, she has not engaged in disordered eating behavior for the past three years. Krystal is married and has three children ages 9, 8, and 5. Krystal and her family are Christian, and they attend church every Sunday. Krystal works as a real-estate agent and her spouse is the manager of a local restaurant. Krystal and her family have always gotten by financially but, given the economic climate as a result of the COVID-19 pandemic, Krystal has been having a difficult time generating enough clients to maintain a consistent income. Her partner's restaurant is not doing well either and they have been close to having to shut the restaurant down three times in the last year. Krystal has been homeschooling her kids, but her middle child was recently diagnosed with ADHD and has struggled a lot with the less structured environment of homeschool. Krystal has been butting heads with her middle child almost daily and has been unsuccessful in finding ways to help manage the needs of all her children. Krystal is beginning to struggle with her faith given the current circumstances, and this is creating tension with her spouse, whose faith is very strong.

Naomi has battled a combination of anorexia and orthorexia since she was a teenager. She has been able to maintain a healthy weight for the past three years but has recently become more rigid with her orthorexia. Naomi has two children, ages 8 and 10. Naomi recently moved in with her partner of four years, and her partner also has two children, ages 14 and 6. Naomi's partner has a volatile relationship with their ex, and they have been in a custody battle for the last two years. This has put a strain on Naomi's relationship with both her partner and her partner's children. Recently, Naomi discovered the 14-year-old has been sneaking out of the house to get drunk and high with friends, and this exacerbated the problems Naomi has been having connecting with the 14-year-old. Naomi also now lives in her partner's house, which is in a very different neighborhood culturally than she is used to. Naomi and her children are an ethnic minority in this new neighborhood, and Naomi worries that her children will stand out too much at their new school and be ostracized because of their cultural differences.

Johanna has had a lifelong battle with obesity and binge eating disorder. She is a new mother, having just delivered her first baby 2 months ago. Johanna's fiancé is in the military and was recently deployed for the first time just a few weeks before their baby was born. About a year prior to the deployment, Johanna and her fiancé moved across the country because the cost of living was so high, and Johanna was having difficulty finding employment. All of Johanna's family and friends live out of state. She recently learned that her father was diagnosed with stage 4 cancer and is not expected to live more than 6 months. This combination of events and lack of available support has contributed to Johanna relapsing with her eating disorder.

Take some time to reflect and journal about your reactions to the narratives you just read. Do you identify with anything in any of these narratives? Do you find yourself being critical or judgmental toward anyone in these narratives? What ecological systems do you think are most at play in each of these narratives?

Chapter 8:
Common Childhood Eating Habits & Concerns

Chapter 8: Common Childhood Eating Habits & Concerns

As you're discovering, the things your children are exposed to influence their behaviors and shape their personality. Therefore, it makes sense that this same principle would apply to food and eating habits. As a general principle, the more you expose your children to a variety of foods, the more open they will be to trying those and other novel foods in the future. Children who are presented with novel foods multiple times are more likely to request those foods later.

Modeling also plays a role in this area. The foods that children observe their parents eating and enjoying are the foods that they gravitate towards as well. Your own eating habits, whether positive or negative, quickly influence the eating habits of your children. This is true for a number of reasons. First of all, the foods that you prefer are the foods that are more likely to be in your home, and consequently are the foods with which your children will be most familiar. Secondly, you're probably eating these foods around your children a lot of the time. This is reinforcing for them because, as their model, they will assume that the foods you eat and enjoy are the foods they should have too.

However, childhood is not without its challenges when it comes to food and eating habits, even if you strive to do everything right when it comes to helping your kid develop healthy eating habits. Having struggled yourself with food, you are probably more in tune and prepared to deal with any challenges your children may have. However, this also means that any food issues that emerge in them can be a trigger for you as well. This is important to be mindful of because food and eating challenges are actually much more common than you might think in children.

Over 75% of children between the ages of 2-4 are particular about the kinds of food they eat, in addition to being picky about what they wear, how they are put to bed, and how things are done. The children who are most likely to develop pickiness in any of these areas include those who have a difficult temperament, have experienced a childhood illness, were born prematurely, exhibit sleeping difficulties, or have developmental disabilities.

Picky eating behaviors typically decline when kids are around age 6, however there are a number of different factors that could contribute to the perpetuation of rigidity and pickiness around food. We'll discuss some of these factors in the sections below. Even so, it is important to emphasize that it does not appear that most kids who are picky eaters or have other eating challenges in childhood are any more likely to develop severe eating-disordered behaviors than non-picky eaters and those without any eating difficulties in childhood.

Autism

Around 70% of autistic children have some form of eating challenge. This can include things like hypersensitivity to texture, limited food preferences, food pocketing (holding food in the mouth for long periods of time without swallowing it), and pica (eating non-food items). Food difficulties in Autistic children tend to center around sensory sensitivities, but interestingly it's more likely that there is an aversion to the texture or smell of a food than there is to how the food tastes. For example, cooked carrots don't have much of a flavor difference compared to raw carrots, but the texture is very different. Alternatively, canned chicken and canned tuna have a very similar appearance and texture, and many would argue that the flavor is similar as well, especially when mixed with other ingredients (like a tuna salad sandwich vs. a chicken salad sandwich), however the smell is very different between the two.

Autistic children tend to also be very rigid when it comes to the foods they eat and the way in which they're prepared. This is often accompanied by an underlying fear or anxiety. Children might refuse to eat "hard" foods or foods that aren't cut into small pieces because they are afraid of choking. Others may refuse to eat foods that have touched each other (meaning they have to be physically separated on their plate), or they may only eat foods that are a particular color, size, or brand. There is often an intense need for "sameness," meaning that foods that are not prepared or served in the same way every time are more likely to be rejected. Let's say you typically cut a turkey and cheese sandwich in half diagonally for your child but today you decide to cut it in half lengthwise. That could be enough to elicit a refusal from your child, even if the sandwich itself has all the same ingredients. A refusal could even come down to something as detailed as the dishes and utensils used. For instance, if your child prefers to eat with a special blue fork and you try offering a red fork instead, that may elicit a refusal to eat.

However, not all unusual food habits and eating behaviors have to do with an aversion. Conversely, there may be a sensory fixation or stimulation at play. For example, some kids who pocket their food are doing it because they like the sensation it has in their mouth. They may also like the way certain foods look, sound, or feel, and may "stim" on those foods with their eyes or hands instead of eating them. Autistic children with pica tend to fall into this category as well, with the item they are eating fulfilling some sort of sensory stimulation. However, pica can also indicate the presence of a nutritional deficiency (zinc and iron deficiencies are common), so it will be important to talk to your child's doctor, especially if your child regularly eats the same non-food item.

While most childhood medical or mental health diagnoses are not associated with higher rates of eating disorders, it is important to note that Autistic individuals as a population do appear to have a higher likelihood of developing rigid eating habits, including Orthorexia, and are more likely to be diagnosed with an eating disorder, specifically Anorexia, later in life. They are also more likely to be diagnosed with ARFID in childhood, which will be described in more detail in the section below. To be clear, this does not mean that all Autistic individuals will develop a more serious eating disorder, but as a population they are at a higher risk than non-Autistic people.

ARFID

ARFID stands for Avoidant/Restrictive Food Intake Disorder. ARFID was designated as an "official" diagnosis in the 5th edition of the Diagnostic and Statistical Manual of Mental Disorders (DSM-5), which was released in 2013. ARFID is most commonly diagnosed in children. ARFID is characterized by a pattern of eating that may include the following:

- Avoiding certain foods or groups of foods entirely. The avoidance may be around a specific type of food, such as a meat or fruit; food with a certain texture, such as any food deemed to be "slimy;" or food that is at a certain temperature, such as refusing to eat any foods that are too hot or too cold.

- Severely restricting the amount of food that is eaten. The restriction occurs to the point that the child loses weight or does not gain weight appropriately, develops a nutritional deficiency, or becomes dependent on enteral feeding (tube feeding) or oral nutrition supplements like pre-packaged protein shakes or powders.

- Gagging or retching at the sight or smell of a particular food. This could be so severe that the child can't even be in the same room as someone who is eating that food.

- Avoidance of social events or a refusal to go anywhere a particular aversive food might be present, such as a restaurant or birthday party.

- Maintaining a diet that is severely limited, containing 10 or fewer foods that are considered "safe" or "preferred."

- Lack of interest in food or intentionally missing meals due to not feeling hungry. It's important to ensure this symptom is not due to other factors. For example, children with ADHD who are taking a stimulant medication tend to experience appetite suppression as a side effect of their medication.

- Struggling to stay and/or eat at the dinner table during meals.

- Only being able to eat when there is a distraction, such as watching tv.

- Developing an extreme fear of negative consequences from eating, such as a fear of choking, vomiting, or experiencing gastrointestinal issues. Here again it's important to ensure there are no other factors in play that could be causing symptoms after eating, such as an undiagnosed food allergy.

- Unlike other eating disorders, people with ARFID do not have a distorted body image or a preoccupation or concern with their weight.

ARFID has been found to be most prevalent in Autistic children, however not all children with ARFID are Autistic, nor do all Autistic children develop ARFID. Children with ADHD, an anxiety disorder, or OCD are also more at risk for developing ARFID, as are children who don't outgrow typical picky eating behaviors and those who have more severe picky eating behaviors.

Food Allergies & Sensitivities

Due to a variety of factors, there are a growing number of children who have food sensitivities or allergies. These may not be immediately apparent because they don't trigger an obvious allergic reaction such as developing hives or triggering anaphylaxis. The most common things for children to be allergic/sensitive to include gluten, dairy (especially casein, a milk protein), corn, eggs, soy, nuts, and fish/shellfish. Many children are also allergic or sensitive to artificial coloring including carmine (red #4), tartazine (FD&C yellow #5), and annatto. Unfortunately, a lot of food contains "hidden" artificial coloring, including frozen meat and fish, soda, juice, yogurt, cake mix, candy, crackers, chips, cereal, processed cheese, jam/jelly, condiments, ice cream, canned fruit, and instant pudding.

Some populations of children are more likely to have food allergies or sensitivities than others. These include children with Autism or ADHD, children diagnosed with ODD or identified as having difficulties with behavioral or emotional regulation, children with Downs Syndrome or other developmental disabilities, children who have other environmental allergies or asthma, and children with epilepsy or a seizure disorder. There has also been growing research that an undetected food sensitivity can exacerbate behavioral and emotional problems and can increase symptoms of anxiety or depression. The good news is that, as food sensitivities are becoming better understood, there is growing accessibility to food sensitivity testing, some of which can even be done on your own at home!

What This Means

When it comes to food, a degree of pickiness or challenging behavior is considered both normal and developmentally appropriate. Just because children are experiencing difficulty with some aspect of food does not mean that there is something wrong with them, nor does it predict that they will have eating-disordered behaviors in the future. Rather, being a picky eater is usually more a manifestation of a developmental stage and is less an indicator of a serious problem. Even in populations of children where abnormal or unusual eating behaviors are more pronounced, these behaviors are typically more a manifestation of aspects of those other diagnoses than they are an indicator that your child has an eating disorder.

However, what has been unequivocally shown to impact children's present and future eating habits are your own eating habits. The foods that you eat are undoubtedly the foods that your children will also eat. The way you interact with food is the way they will learn to interact with food. Their food preferences will be based on the degree to which they're exposed to or restricted from a variety of foods. This means you will need to be very mindful of your relationship with food and how you talk about food in front of your child.

How Your Eating Disorder Affects Your Child's Relationship with Food

As someone who has had an eating disorder, you have probably struggled with varying degrees of selectivity surrounding the foods you will and will not eat. You may have based food preferences on caloric value, grams of fat, or on the ease with which you could eliminate them from your body. Regardless of what your motivation was, chances are strong that you developed some unhealthy eating habits. Aside from the restrictions you put on yourself regarding what you ate, at one point or another you likely engaged in maladaptive rituals or habits surrounding mealtimes as well. This may have included combining foods that don't typically go together, cutting your food into tiny pieces before eating anything, prohibiting certain food items from touching others, eating only at specific times or under specific circumstances (i.e., only when you were alone), etc.

It's important to acknowledge the growing emphasis over the past few years on the benefit of a "whole-foods" diet, where processed foods, refined sugars, and foods that commonly cause inflammation or other gut issues are significantly reduced or eliminated. Popular diets include Paleo, Ketogenic, and Whole30. The premise of these diets is well-founded by science, and the principle of eating clean and being educated on the impact "unhealthy" foods have on your body can be beneficial, especially if it turns out you have underlying food allergies or sensitivities. However, strict adherence to this way of eating has contributed to the emergence of Orthorexia and the perpetuation of rigid eating habits. This rigidity even goes against the principles behind most of the whole-foods diets, where an 80-20 compliance rate is encouraged for those who don't have significant food allergies or complex reactions to foods that are not typically a part of these diets. This approach encourages people to fully comply with the diet 80% of the time and to allow exceptions 20% of the time. If you consider the average person eats 3 meals a day, this ratio allows for about 4 meals each week to include foods that are not a part of the standard diet.

If you expose your children to any of the above-mentioned eating patterns, they run an increased risk of developing the same patterns. Again, this isn't necessarily because they are developing an eating disorder, but rather because they are designed to model their behavior after yours. It really is a "monkey-see, monkey-do" kind of phenomenon. As their mom, they see you as the example, the one who knows what is good and bad for them. They automatically perceive the things you do as being good and therefore as the things they should be doing too.

If you are the parent of a child with special, complex, or different needs, it's important to be mindful that you could be triggered given your eating disorder history. For example, if you have struggled with Anorexia and go on to have an Autistic child who is a severely picky eater and is later diagnosed with ARFID, you may struggle to know how to appropriately navigate that in a way that won't trigger your own tendencies to restrict or avoid certain foods. If you struggle with Orthorexia and have eliminated all gluten because of a rigidity vs. a true health issue, and you then go on to have a child that's diagnosed with Celiac Disease, you may find it challenging to differentiate between the very real medical needs of your child vs. your own obsession with eating gluten-free.

Regardless of where you are in your recovery, it will be very important for you to monitor your eating habits around your children, as well as any negative talk about food. If you're going to engage in behaviors or speak negatively about food in any way, do it away from the presence of your children. If you have a child with special needs, you will very likely need some extra support around you to help monitor your own recovery. And, as always, it is important that you be willing to bring these things up with your therapist.

What You Can Do

Make the choice to establish balanced eating habits with your children. Even if you're still in a place of working on this for yourself, it is possible to successfully expose your children to an appropriate relationship with food. However, if you feel that you're really not in the place in your recovery where you can do this for them yourself, make sure they spend ample time around those who can. Expose them to well-balanced, homemade meals whenever possible, and if they're old enough, let them help you out in the kitchen as the meal is being prepared. This way they will learn practical and fun ways to interact with food, aside from just consuming it. Having sit-down dinners with the entire family on a consistent basis will also create a positive association with food for your children, because it will remind them of time spent with loved ones.

If you have a child with special or divergent needs, you may need to do things differently than you would for a typical child. This is true for most aspects of parenting, but the focus here is on how you help your child navigate their relationship with food. If you have a child who is extremely picky, anxious, or aversive to any food, the most important thing to do initially is to rule out any possible medical problems. Children who are refusing to eat may be experiencing gastrointestinal distress from a specific food.

If medical issues and food allergies/sensitivities have been ruled out, you can now be more certain that there is some other sensory or psychological reason why your child is being picky, rigid, or restrictive. When working with children to become more flexible in their eating patterns, the first and most important thing to do in this situation is to keep your own emotions in check, staying as calm and patient as possible whenever you are interacting with your child around food.

It's important to remember that it can easily take over a dozen exposures to a particular food before a child may be willing to try it. If, however, you have attempted a food a handful of times and you are still not having success in getting your child to eat it, there are some things you should be asking yourself to ensue you are not continuing to push it out of your own disordered eating thoughts or rigidities:

- Is this specific food essential? When you think "essential," think about water. If we don't drink water, we will die. However, there are very few foods that carry this same level of importance as water does. Your children will not die if they go their entire lives without eating broccoli.

- What nutrients does this particular food provide? Are there other foods that also have these nutrients that your child does eat or may be more willing to eat than the food you are currently trying? Most people would agree that nutrients like vitamin C and Omega-3 are important to have in our diet, and most would also agree that having a balance of macro- and micro-nutrients is ideal. However, that doesn't mean you need to try and force your kids to eat bell peppers (a food very high in vitamin C) if they are willing to eat other foods high in vitamin C, like kiwis. If you aren't sure which foods contain which nutrients, it may be helpful to consult with a nutritionist or dietitian for some ideas and guidance.

When moving forward with trying to get children to try a food they are initially averse to or uncertain about, remember to take small steps toward tasting the food. First, if they are willing, allow them to explore the food with their other senses. Let them look at it, smell it, and touch it (yes, even it makes a mess!). You can then move toward things like giving it a "kiss" or licking it before finally having them put it in their mouth, chewing it, and swallowing it. Mixing a new food with an already known and preferred food can sometimes help this process.

Being mindful of textures will be especially important for children who are Autistic or have ARFID. For example, many children do not like the texture of raw tomatoes, however if tomatoes are blended into a sauce or soup, or if they are chopped up finely and mixed with other ingredients to make a salsa, your child may be more receptive to trying it. You could also try the same food prepared in different ways, such as having your child try mashed potatoes, French fries, and baked potatoes with fixings.

Autonomy and choice will be your best friends when working to get children to eat more foods. Remember that a drive for control is a big component of a variety of mental and emotional disorders, so as much as possible you will need to give them the perception that they have control and choice whenever possible. If you want your children to eat more vegetables, offer a choice of 3-5 vegetables and let them pick what they want. Better yet (if you have the time and resources to do this) give them some of all 3-5 vegetables and allow them to choose what they eat.

One thing to be particularly mindful of is the use of rewards to get children to eat something. This may be very tempting to do, especially because this is often a successful way to get them to eat something. However, if they genuinely do not like the food and are only eating it to get rewarded or praised, that is setting them up for an inappropriate relationship with food. This is especially true if you use desserts or other "special" foods to bribe children to eat their "regular" food. This serves to place foods into inappropriate, separate categories rather than helping them learn how to healthily balance the variety of foods. It also further perpetuates the rigid categorization of "safe" vs. "unsafe" foods.

Finally, it is important to remember that there will be some foods your children simply do not like... and that is ok! As an adult, you likely have your own food preferences (separate from disordered eating behaviors), and your children are no different. The best you can do is try and keep their meals as balanced as possible. However, if you have tried a particular food numerous times and your child is still refusing to eat it, it is probably best for everyone's well-being to move on.

One of the worst things you can do, especially for children with divergent needs, is put an aversive food in front of them and either force them to sit there until they eat it or refuse to let them eat anything else until they eat that one food. With neurotypical children, you may eventually be able to break their will down enough that they'll eat the food. Neurotypical children who are picky eaters will not starve themselves, however some neurodiverse children will.

Reflections

1. What are some unhealthy or disordered thoughts and behaviors you have developed specifically surrounding food or food combinations? Are you currently struggling with any of these?

2. What was the most difficult part of your disordered eating habits to give up? This may have been a specific food combination, a ritual surrounding mealtime, rigidity surrounding when and how you ate, etc. Why do you think this particular thing was so difficult for you?

3. What eating difficulties (if any) does your child currently display? What thoughts and feelings are evoked in you whenever your child experiences these difficulties?

4. Do you and/or your child have any special or diverse needs? If so, how do you find that your/their neurodiversity contributes to your/their eating habits and preferences? How does that neurodiversity impact the parent-child relationship?

Application

If you have children who are particularly picky about what they eat, you may have discovered that trying to force or coerce them into eating things rarely works. Instead, try approaching the issue from a more interactive method. This will look differently depending on the age of your child.

For babies and young toddlers, use the modeling approach to your advantage. Remember that whatever they see you do, they will do. If they seem unwilling or skeptical about trying a certain food, be overly exuberant in your reaction to the food. If you eat or pretend to eat some of their food, this will add to their buy-in. Even if this is a feigned interest on your part, your kids will likely respond to your positive reaction and develop at least a curiosity about the food.

For older ones, you could even turn this into a game: pretend that you like their food so much that you make multiple attempts to "steal" some from them before they can get to it. The goal of this game is to get them to "protect" their food and eat it before you do. Of course, you will want to make sure they are doing this safely (not eating too fast, chewing well before swallowing, etc.).

If your children are a little bit older, you might be able to entice them to try new foods by turning it into a detective game. Have a couple of different foods hidden under plates or napkins. Make them close their eyes and use their other senses to solve the mystery of what the food is. See if they can figure it out by smelling it and touching it. Once they have a hypothesis, the final test is for them to taste it to see if they guessed correctly.

If mealtimes are a struggle for your children, start thinking outside the box. Food doesn't always have to be served at the kitchen table. Think about incorporating the meal into other settings or activities. Take your children on a picnic lunch to a park or zoo, or even just in your own back yard. Have dinner out at a favorite restaurant on occasion. Sometimes all it really takes is a change of scenery to encourage a new attitude toward food.

If your children are old enough, allow them to be a part of preparing meals. Even three- and four-year-olds can help with things like setting the table, tearing lettuce, buttering bread, stirring a pot with supervision, etc. For older children and pre-teens, consider buying a children's cookbook and let them pick out recipes to make. If they are part of creating the meal and are given praise for their work, they likely will feel a sense of pride and accomplishment. This in turn will make them more willing to try the food, because they will probably be curious about what they helped prepare. You could even allow your children to be a part of planning the meal once or twice a week. If you want them to try something new, allowing them to choose a preferred side dish, entrée, or dessert to go along with the novel dish may increase their willingness to try it. Think about how much the element of control factors into this. As a fighter of an eating disorder, you know better than most how important control can be. If your children feel like they get to be in control of some of the things surrounding their meal, they are less likely to resist your control in other things.

Narratives

Cassandra has a history of Anorexia and Orthorexia. She has her eating habits mostly under control and in a healthy place, but she also has periods of time where she struggles. This tends to happen the most around her biggest "fear" foods, which include pizza and ice cream. Cassandra is typically able to eat her "fear" foods at this point in her recovery, however she still has some disordered habits including cutting pizza slices into even smaller slices and taking off all the toppings and eating them separately and waiting for her ice cream to be almost fully melted before eating it. Cassandra has a 9-year-old daughter. Recently, Cassandra took her daughter to a friend's birthday party, and it just so happened they were serving pizza. Cassandra watched in embarrassment as her daughter, after being served a slice of pizza, insisted it was too big and demanded smaller pieces. She then watched her daughter take off all the toppings, separate them by topping, and eat them separately after she ate the pizza slice.

Mila has been in recovery from Binge Eating Disorder for about 5 years. She has a 7-year-old son who has grown increasingly picky in his food preferences. Her son used to be a very adventurous eater, but he has grown more particular as he's gotten older. It has gotten to the point where he will only eat a handful of things, and the few things he will eat have to be a specific brand or prepared in a very specific way. This has been a challenge for Mila, as she has always loved meal times and enjoys trying new and different foods and recipes. Mila tends to become very reactive when her son won't try something new, and at times she has punished him for not trying something she wanted him to. Mila eventually gives in and lets her son eat what he wants, but they both end up getting upset and there is a palpable tension that exists around mealtimes.

Beverly has a history of bulimic and orthorexic traits, however she has never been officially diagnosed or received treatment outside of working sporadically with a therapist in outpatient therapy. Beverly has a history of researching different diet trends, and she has tried several over the years. Beverly tends to become overly rigid in her adherence to these diets. On the rare occasion that she eats something that is not an acceptable food within that diet, she purges it. Beverly has a 3-year-old son who has been struggling with mysterious gastrointestinal issues. After taking him to several specialists, it is discovered that he has a gluten sensitivity. Beverly finds herself experiencing a lot of relief, in part because she now knows what is going on for her son, but also in part because one of the rigidities Beverly has developed has been in eliminating all gluten from her diet. Beverly had her own food sensitivity testing done after her son was diagnosed, and she was found to not have a strong sensitivity or reaction to gluten. Despite this, and despite the fact that her son's doctor has told Beverly her son can have small amounts of gluten, especially if it organic and not genetically modified, Beverly has maintained 100% adherence to a gluten-free diet for both herself and her son.

Ciana has been in recovery from Anorexia for 10 years. She has a 5-year-old daughter who was recently diagnosed with Autism. Her daughter has developed increasingly odd behaviors around food. Ciana has noticed her daughter seems to have intense emotional reactions to food. For the food she likes, Ciana's daughter is very particular around how it is prepared and served. She has a meltdown if different foods are touching or if there is not an equal amount of each food item on her plate. She also seems to have an intense fear and aversion toward certain foods, refusing to eat anything that is too "hard" because she is afraid of choking, and refusing to eat raw tomatoes and deli meat because they are too "slimy." Ciana is finding herself getting very triggered by her daughter's behaviors, as they remind her a lot of similar behaviors she engaged in when she was deep into her eating disorder. She has reacted strongly toward her daughter's behaviors at times because of this, but this only seems to escalate her daughter even further and she becomes even more rigid and insistent. Things have gotten so bad that Ciana is sometimes unable to remain in the room with her daughter during mealtimes because of how triggered she gets. She has started to rely heavily on her partner to feed their daughter.

Take some time to reflect and journal about your reactions to the narratives you just read. Who do you most identify with? Who do you feel most critical or judgmental toward? Which children, if any, would you identify as having significant eating issues? Which children, if any, would you identify as having developmentally typical behavior?

Concluding Remarks & Statements

It should be recognized that your willingness and dedication to work through this book speaks volumes about the type of mother you are. The fact that you have struggled with disordered eating, poor body image, low self-esteem, control issues, anxiety, and or/depression is a clue to the difficult life you have led. Eating disorders and other mental health struggles do not take place inside of a vacuum. While there are many factors that come into play, it's likely that many of the things that were addressed in this manual with regards to your children's developmental and emotional needs were left unmet or unfulfilled for you in your own life.

Women with eating disorders are more likely than non-eating-disordered women to have had insecure attachments to their parents. You also likely were met with resistance when you tried to separate and individuate from your parents. Additionally, chances are high that your own mother had disordered eating behaviors and that she made negative comments about both herself and about your own weight or appearance. It's also more likely that you were sexually abused at some point in your childhood. Eating disorders occur within a vicious familial cycle and they have been shown to span across many generations at times.

By reading this book and engaging yourself in this process, you have come one step closer to breaking that cycle for good. You have had a lot of things stacked against you, yet somehow you have made the choice to fight against it all and make a better life for both yourself and for your children. For that, you are to be commended. My wish is that this book provided you with a newfound sense of hope and encouragement to do the things you need to do to make a better life for your children and for yourself. There aren't many people who deserve a chance to start a new cycle more than you do. Take it and boldly run with it!

References

Abbassi, A., & Aslinia, S. (2010). Family violence, trauma, and social learning theory. *Journal of Professional Counseling: Practice, Theory, & Research, 38,* 16-27.

Abraham, S., Taylor, A., Conti, J. (2001). Postnatal depression, eating, exercise, and vomiting before and during pregnancy. *International Journal of Eating Disorders, 29,* 482-487.

Ainsworth, M., & Bell, S. (1970). Attachment, exploration, and separation: Illustrated by the behavior of one-year-olds in a strange situation. *Child Development, 41,* 49-67.

Ainsworth, M., Blehar, M., Walters, E., & Wall, S. (1978). *Patterns of attachment: A psychological study of the strange situation.* Hillsdale, NJ: Lawrence Erlbaum Associates.

Akers, R. (1998). *Social learning and social structure: A general theory of crime and deviance.* Boston, MA: Northeastern University Press.

Ali E. (2018). Women's experiences with postpartum anxiety disorders: A narrative literature review. *International Journal of Women's Health, 10,* 237–249.

American Psychiatric Association (2000). *Diagnostic and statistical manual of mental disorders* (4th ed., text revision). Washington, DC: Author.

Ante, Z, Luu, T., Healy-Profitós, J., He, S., Taddeo, D., Lo, E., & Auger, N. (2020). Pregnancy outcomes in women with anorexia nervosa. *International Journal of Eating Disorders, 53,* 403-412.

Arnold, L., Lofthouse, N. & Hurt, E. (2012). Artificial food colors and attention-deficit/hyperactivity symptoms: Conclusions to dye for. *Neurotherapeutics, 9*, 599–609.

Ausderau, K. & Juarez, M. (2013). The impact of autism spectrum disorders and eating challenges on family mealtimes. *ICAN: Infant, Child, & Adolescent Nutrition, 5,* 315-323.

Bade, M., Rammeloo, E., Hermans, J., de Vries Locher, A., de Graaf, E., & Mearin, M. (1995). Symptoms of disease and food allergy in children with Down syndrome. *Nederlands Tijdschrift Voor Geneeskunde, 139*, 1680–1684.

Bandura, A. (1965). Influence of models' reinforcement contingencies on the acquisition of imitative responses. *Journal of Personality and Social Psychology, 1,* 589-595.

Bandura, A. (1971). *Psychological modeling: Conflicting theories.* New Brunswick, NJ: Transaction Publishers.

Bandura, A. (1977). *Social learning theory.* Upper Saddle River, NJ: Prentice Hall.

Bandura, A. (1986). *Social foundations of thought and action: A social cognitive theory.* Englewood Cliffs, NJ: Prentice Hall.

Bandura, A., Ross, D., & Ross, S. (1963). A comparative test of the status envy, social power, and secondary reinforcement theories of identificatory learning. *Journal of Abnormal and Social Psychology, 67,* 527-534.

Baron-Cohen, S., Jaffa, T., Davies, S., Auyeung, B., Allison, C., & Wheelwrright, S. (2013). Do girls with anorexia nervosa have elevated autistic traits? *Molecular Autism, 4,*

Benedikt, R., Wertheim, E., & Love, A. (1998). Eating attitudes and weight-loss attempts in female adolescents and their mothers. *Journal of Youth and Adolescence, 27,* 43-57.

Berger, K. (2003). *The developing person through childhood and adolescence* (6th ed.). New York, NY: Worth Publishers.

Birch, L., & Marlin, D. (1982). I don't like it; I never tried it: Effects of exposure on two-year-old children's food preferences. *Appetite, 3,* 353-360.

Blackmore, E., Côté-Arsenault, D., Tang, W., Glover, V., Evans, J., Golding, J., & O'Connor, T. (2011). Previous prenatal loss as a predictor of perinatal depression and anxiety. *The British Journal of Psychiatry: The Journal of Mental Science, 198,* 373–378.

Bodiford McNeil, C. & Hembree-Kigin, T. (2010). *Parent-Child Interaction Therapy.* (2nd ed.). New York, NY: Springer Science + Business Media, LLC.

Bowlby, J. (1979). *The making and breaking of affectional bonds.* London, UK: Tavistock Publications Limited.

Bowlby, J. (1982). *Attachment and loss volume I: Attachment* (2nd ed.). New York, NY: Basic Books.

Bowen, M. (1978). *Family therapy in clinical practice.* New York, NY: Jason Aronson.

Broberg, A., Hjalmers, I., & Nevonen, L. (2001). Eating disorders, attachment and interpersonal difficulties: A comparison between 18- to 24-year-old patients and normal controls. *European Eating Disorders Review, 9, 381-396.*

Bronfenbrenner, U. (1979). *The ecology of human development.* Cambridge, MA: Harvard University Press.

Bryant-Waugh, R., Turner, H., Jones, C., & Gamble, C. (2007). Developing a parenting skills-and-support intervention for mothers with eating disorders and pre-school children part 2: Piloting a group intervention. *European Eating Disorders Review, 15,* 439-448.

Bratman, S. (1997). Health food junkie. *Yoga Journal, 136.* 42–50.

Bratman S. (2017). Orthorexia vs. theories of healthy eating. *Eating and Weight Disorders: EWD, 22*, 381–385.

Brennan, K., Clark, C., & Shaver, P. (1998). Self-report measurement of adult attachment: An integrative overview. In J. A. Simpson & W. S. Rholes (Eds.), *Attachment Theory and Close Relationships* (pp. 46–76). The Guilford Press.

Bulik, C., Von Holle, A., Siega-Riz, A., Torgesen, L., Lie, K., Hamer, R., Reichborn-Kjennerud, T. (2009). Birth outcomes in women with eating disorders in the Norwegian Mother and Child Cohort Study (MoBa). *International Journal of Eating Disorders, 42,* 9-18.

Butler, A., Van Lieshout, R., Lipman, E., MacMillan, H., Gonzalez, A., Gorter, J., Georgiades, K., Speechley, K., Boyle, M., & Ferro, M. (2018). Mental disorder in children with physical conditions: a pilot study. *BMJ Open, 8.*

Cachelin, F., Schug, R., Juarez, L. & Monreal, T. (2005). Sexual abuse and eating disorders in a community sample of Mexican American women. *Hispanic Journal of Behavioral Sciences, 27,* 533-546.

Carter, J., Bewell, C., Blackmore, E., & Woodside, D. (2006). The impact of childhood sexual abuse in anorexia nervosa. *Child Abuse & Neglect: The International Journal, 30,* 257-269.

Cena, H., Barthels, F., Cuzzolaro, M., Bratman, S., Brytek-Matera, A., Dunn, T., Varga, M., Missbach, B., & Donini, L. M. (2019). Definition and diagnostic criteria for orthorexia nervosa: a narrative review of the literature. *Eating and Weight Disorders: EWD, 24,* 209–246.

Charbonneau, K. & Seabrook, J. (2019). Adverse birth outcomes associated with types of eating disorders: A review. *Canadian Journal of Dietetic Practice and Research, 80,* 131-136.

Cole-Detke, H., & Kobak, R. (1996). Attachment processes in eating disorder and depression. *Journal of Consulting and Clinical Psychology, 64,* 282-290.

Crowell, J. & Treboux, D. (1995) A review of adult attachment measures: Implications for theory and research. *Social Development, 4,* 294-327.

Davison, K., Markey, C., & Birch, L. (2000). Etiology of body dissatisfaction and weight concerns among 5-year-old girls. *Appetite, 35,* 143-151.

Dickerson Mayes, S. & Zickgraf, H. (2019). Atypical eating behaviors in children and adolescents with autism, ADHD, other disorders, and typical development. *Research in Autism Spectrum Disorders, 64,* 76-83.

Dunn, T. M., & Bratman, S. (2016). On orthorexia nervosa: A review of the literature and proposed diagnostic criteria. *Eating Behaviors, 21,* 11–17.

Erikson, E. (1963). *Childhood and society* (2nd ed.). New York, NY: Norton.

Evans, D., Leckman, J., Carter, A., Reznick, J., Henshaw, D., King, R., & Pauls, D. (1997). Ritual, habit, and perfectionism: The prevalence and development of compulsive-like behavior in normal young children, *Child Development, 68*, 58-68.

Eyberg, S. & Funderburk, B. (2011). *Parent-Child Interaction Therapy Protocol.* PCIT International.

Farr, S., Dietz, P., O'Hara, M., Burley, K., & Ko, J. (2014). Postpartum anxiety and comorbid depression in a population-based sample of women. *Journal of Women's Health, 23,* 120–128.

Feeney, J., Noller, P., & Callan, V. (1994). Attachment style, communication and satisfaction in the early years of marriage. In K. Bartholomew & D. Perlman (Eds.), *Attachment Processes in Adulthood* (pp. 269–308). Jessica Kingsley Publishers.

Feodor Nilsson, S., Andersen, P. K., Strandberg-Larsen, K., & Nybo Andersen, A. M. (2014). Risk factors for miscarriage from a prevention perspective: a nationwide follow-up study. *BJOG: An International Journal of Obstetrics and Gynaecology, 12,* 1375–1384.

Fisher, M. M., Rosen, D. S., Ornstein, R. M., Mammel, K. A., Katzman, D. K., Rome, E. S., Callahan, S. T., Malizio, J., Kearney, S., & Walsh, B. T. (2014). Characteristics of avoidant/restrictive food intake disorder in children and adolescents: a "new disorder" in DSM-5. *The Journal of Adolescent Health: Official Publication of the Society for Adolescent Medicine, 55*, 49–52.

Fraley, R. (2002). Attachment stability from infancy to adulthood: Meta-analysis and dynamic modeling of developmental mechanisms. *Personality and Social Psychology Review, 6,* 123–151.

Fraley, R. & Davis, K. (1997). Attachment formation and transfer in young adults' close friendships and romantic relationships. *Personal Relationships, 4*, 131–144.

Fraley, R. & Shaver, P. (1997). Adult attachment and the suppression of unwanted thoughts. *Journal of Personality and Social Psychology, 73*, 1080–1091.

Fraley, R. & Shaver, P. (2000). Adult romantic attachment: Theoretical developments, emerging controversies, and unanswered questions. *Review of General Psychology, 4,* 132-154.

Fraley, R. & Spieker, S. (2003). Are infant attachment patterns continuously or categorically distributed? A taxometric analysis of strange situation behavior. *Developmental Psychology, 39*, 387–404.

Fraley, R. & Waller, N. (1998). Adult attachment patterns: A test of the typological model. In J. A. Simpson & W. S. Rholes (Eds.), *Attachment Theory and Close Relationships* (pp. 77–114). The Guilford Press.

Fraley, R., Waller, N., & Brennan, K. (2000). An item response theory analysis of self-report measures of adult attachment. *Journal of Personality and Social Psychology, 78,* 350–365.

Franko, D., Blais, M., Becker, A., Delinsky, S., Greenwood, D., Flores, A., & Herzog, D. (2001). Pregnancy complications and neonatal outcomes in women with eating disorders. *American Journal of Psychiatry, 158,* 1461-1466.

Frazier, T., Hogue, C., Bonney, E., Yount, K., & Pearce, B. (2018). Weathering the storm; a review of pre-pregnancy stress and risk of spontaneous abortion. *Psychoneuroendocrinology, 92,* 142–154.

Giannandrea, S., Cerulli, C., Anson, E., & Chaudron, L. (2013). Increased risk for postpartum psychiatric disorders among women with past pregnancy loss. *Journal of Women's Health, 22,* 760–768.

Gulotta C., Piazza, C., Patel, M., & Layer S. (2005). Using food redistribution to reduce packing in children with severe food refusal. *Journal of Applied Behavior Analysis, 38,* 39–50.

Hagekull, B., Bohlin, G., & Rydell, A. (1997). Maternal sensitivity, infant temperament, and the development of early feeding problems. *Infant Mental Health Journal, 18*, 92–106.

Hazan, C., & Shaver, P. (1987). Romantic love conceptualized as an attachment process. *Journal of Personality and Social Psychology, 52*, 511–524.

Hoyert, D. & Gregory, E. (2016) Cause of fetal death: Data from the fetal death report, 2014. *National Vital Statistics Reports, 65,* 1-25.

Hudson, J., Hiripi, E., Pope, H., & Kessler, R. (2007). The prevalence and correlates of eating disorders in the national comorbidity survey replication. *Biological Psychiatry, 61,* 348-358.

Huggins, K., Petok, E., & Mireles, O. (2000). Markers of lactation insufficiency: a study of 34 mothers. *Current Issues in Clinical Lactation,* 25-35.

Huke, V., Turk, J., Saeidi, S., Kent, A., & Morgan, J. (2013). Autism spectrum disorders in eating disorder populations: A systematic review. *European Eating Disorders Review: The Journal of the Eating Disorders Association, 21,* 345–351.

Jacobi, C., Schmitz, G., & Agras, W. (2008). Is picky eating an eating disorder? *International Journal of Eating Disorders, 41,* 626-634.

Johnson, R. & Harris, G. (2004). A preliminary study of the predictors of feeding problems in late infancy. *Journal of Reproductive and Infant Psychology, 22,* 183-188.

Kalyva, E. (2008). Comparison of eating attitudes between adolescent girls with and without Asperger syndrome: Daughters' and mothers' reports. *Journal of Autism and Developmental Disorders, 39,* 480-486.

Kenney, L. & Walsh, T. (2013). Avoidant/restrictive food intake disorder (ARFID). *Eating Disorders Review, 24.*

Kenny, M., & Hart, K. (1992). Relationship between parental attachment and eating disorders in an inpatient and a college sample. *Journal of Counseling Psychology, 39,* 521-526.

Kobylewski, S., Jacobson, M., & Center for Science in the Public Interest. (2010). *Food dyes: A rainbow of risks.* Washington, D.C: Center for Science in the Public Interest.

Kobylewski, S. & Jacobson, M. (2012). Toxicology of food dyes. *International Journal of Occupational and Environmental Health, 18,* 220–246.

Kochanska, G., Coy, K., & Murray, K. (2001). The development of self-regulation in the first four years of life. *Child Development, 72,* 1091-1111.

Koubaa, S., Hallstrom, T., Lindholm, C., & Hirschberg, A. (2005). Pregnancy and neonatal outcomes in women with eating disorders. *Obstetrics and Gynecology, 105,* 255-260.

Lacey, J., & Smith, G. (1987) Bulimia nervosa: The impact of pregnancy on mother and baby. *British Journal of Psychiatry, 150,* 777.

Latzer, Y., Hochdorf, Z., Bachar, E., & Canetti, L. (2002). Attachment style and family functioning as discriminating factors in eating disorders. *Contemporary Family Therapy, 24,* 581-599.

Lemberg, R., & Phillips, J. (1989). The impact of pregnancy on anorexia & bulimia nervosa. *International Journal of Eating Disorders, 8,* 285-295.

Lewis, L., & le Grange, D. (1994). The experience and impact of pregnancy in bulimia nervosa: A series of case studies. *European Eating Disorders Review, 2,* 93-105.

Loth, K., Neumark-Sztainer, D., & Croll, J. (2009). Informing family approaches to eating disorder prevention: Perspectives of those who have been there. *International Journal of Eating Disorders, 42,* 146-152.

MacDorman, M., Kirmeyer, S., & Wilson, E. (2012). Fetal and perinatal mortality, United States, 2006. *National Vital Statistics Reports, 60,* 1-23

Mahler, M. (1966). On human symbiosis and the vicissitudes of individuation. *Journal of the American Psychoanalytic Association, 15,* 740-763.

Marsden, P., Meyer, C., Fuller, M., & Waller, G. (2002). The relationship between eating psychopathology and separation-individuation in young nonclinical women. *Journal of Nervous and Mental Disease, 190,* 710-713.

Mars, I. (2012). *"Picky eaters" will not starve themselves but problem or resistant eaters might.* Speech, Language, Feeding.
https://www.speechlanguagefeeding.com/picky-eaters-will-not-starve-themselves-but-problem-or-resistant-eaters-might/

Mayseless, O., & Scharf, M. (2009). Too close for comfort: Inadequate boundaries with parents and individuation in late adolescent girls. *American Journal of Orthopsychiatry, 79,* 191-202.

Mazzeo, S., Slof-Op't Landt, I., Jones, I., Mitchell, K., Kendler, K., & Bulik, C. (2006). Associations among postpartum depression, eating disorders, and perfectionism in a population-based sample of adult women. *International Journal of Eating Disorders, 39,* 202-211.

McNeil, C., & Hembree-Kigin, T. (2011). *Parent-Child Interaction Therapy: Issues in clinical child psychology.* New York, NY: Springer Publishing.

Menella, J., & Beauchamp, G. (1996). Developmental changes in the infants' acceptance of protein-hydrolysate formula and its relation to mothers' eating habits. *Journal of Developmental and Behavioral Pediatrics, 17,* 386-391.

Menella, J., & Beauchamp, G. (1998). Early flavor experiences: Research update. *Nutrition Reviews, 56,* 205-211.

Menella, J. & Beauchamp, G. (2002). Flavor experiences during formula feeding are related to preferences during childhood. *Early Human Development, 68,* 71-82.

Menella, J., & Beauchamp, G. (2004). Flavor programming during infancy. *Pediatrics, 113,* 840-845.

Messner, A., Lalakea, M., Aby, J., Macmahon, J., & Bair, E. (2000). Ankyloglossia: incidence and associated feeding difficulties. *Archives of Otolaryngology--Head & Neck Surgery, 126,* 36-39.

Meyer, D., & Russell, R. (1998). Caretaking, separation from parents, and the development of eating disorders. *Journal of Counseling & Development, 76,* 166-173.

Micali, N., Simonoff, E., & Treasure, J. (2011). Pregnancy and post-partum depression and anxiety in a longitudinal general population cohort: The effect of eating disorders and past depression. *Journal of Affective Disorders, 131,* 150-157.

Mills, N., Pransky, S., Geddes, D., & Mirjalili, S. (2019). What is a tongue tie? Defining the anatomy of the in-situ lingual frenulum. *Clinical Anatomy, 32,* 749-761.

Morgan J., Lacey, J., & Sedgwick P. (1999). Impact of pregnancy on bulimia nervosa. *British Journal of Psychiatry, 174,* 135.

Neifert, M., Seacat, J., & Jobe, W. (1985). Lactation failure due to insufficient glandular development of the breast. *Pediatrics, 76,* 823-828.

Nelson, B., Martin, R., Hodge, S., Havill, V., & Kamphaus, R. (1999). Modeling the prediction of elementary school adjustment from preschool temperament. *Personality and Individual Differences, 26,* 687-700.

Newman, J., Noel, A., Chen, R., & Matsopoulos, A. (1998). Temperament, selected moderating variables, and early reading achievement. *Journal of School Psychology, 36*, 215-232.

O'Dowd, S., & Chang, D. (2017) What is the relationship between anorexia nervosa and miscarriage? *Evidence-Based Practice, 20*, E4.

Oldershaw, A., Treasure, J., Hambrook, D., Tchanturia, K., & Schmidt, U. (2011). Is anorexia nervosa a version of autism spectrum disorders? *European Eating Disorders Review: The Journal of the Eating Disorders Association, 19*, 462–474.

Parry-Jones, B., & Parry-Jones, W. L. (1992). Pica: Symptom or eating disorder? A historical assessment. *The British Journal of Psychiatry: The Journal of Mental Science, 160*, 341–354.

Patel M., Piazza C., Layer, S., Coleman, R., & Swartzwelder, D. (2005). A systematic evaluation of food textures to decrease packing and increase oral intake in children with pediatric feeding disorders. *Journal of Applied Behavior Analysis, 38,* 89–100.

Patel M., Piazza C., Santana C., & Volkert V. (2002). An evaluation of food type and texture in the treatment of a feeding problem. *Journal of Applied Behavior Analysis, 35*, 183–186.

Pelco, L., & Reed-Victor, E. (2003). Understanding and supporting differences in child temperament: Strategies for early childhood environments. *Young Exceptional Children, 6,* 2-11.

Pike, K., & Rodin, J. (1991). Mothers, daughters, and disordered eating. *Journal of Abnormal Psychology, 100,* 198-204.

Pliner, P. (1982). The effects of mere exposure on liking for edible substances. *Appetite, 3,* 283-290.

Qu, F. Wu, Y., Zhu, Y., Barry, J., Ding, T., Baio, G., Muscat, R., Todd, B., Wang, F., & Hardiman, P. (2017). The association between psychological stress and miscarriage: A systematic review and meta-analysis. *Scientific Reports, 7,* 1731.

Reba-Harrelson, L., Von Holle, A., Hamer, R., Torgersen, L., Reichborn-Kjennerud, T., & Bulik, C. (2010). Patterns of maternal feeding and child eating associated with eating disorders in the Norwegian Mother and Child Cohort Study (MoBa). *Eating Behaviors, 11,* 54-61.

Ringer, F. & McKinsey Crittenden, P. (2007). Eating disorders and attachment: The effects of hidden family processes on eating disorders. *European Eating Disorders Review, 15,* 119-130.

Robinson G. (2014). Pregnancy loss. *Best Practice & Research: Clinical Obstetrics & Gynaecology, 28,* 169-178.

Rothbart, M., & Bates, J. (1998). Temperament. In William Damon (Series Ed.), & Nancy Eisenberg (Vol. Ed.), *Handbook of child psychology:* Vol. 3. *Social, emotional, and personality development* (5th ed., pp. 105-176). Hoboken, NJ: John Wiley & Sons.

Schwartz, J., Thigpen, S., & Montgomery, J. (2006). Examination of parenting styles of processing emotions and differentiation of self. *The Family Journal: Counseling and Therapy for Couples and Families, 14,* 41-48.

Sharp, W., Berry, R., McCracken, C., Saulnier, C., Klin, A., Jones, W., & Jacques, D. (2013). Feeding problems and nutrient intake in children with autism spectrum disorders: A meta-analysis and comprehensive review of the literature. *Journal of Autism and Developmental Disorders, 43,* 2159–2173.

Shea, E. (2015). *Supporting autistic people with eating difficulties.* National Autistic Society. https://www.autism.org.uk/advice-and-guidance/professional-practice/autism-eating

Simons, R., Wu, C., Johnson, C., & Conger, R. (1995). A test of various perspectives on the intergenerational transmission of domestic violence. *Criminology, 33,* 141-171.

Simpson, J. & Rholes, W. (2012). Adult attachment orientations, stress, and romantic relationships. *Advances in Experimental Social Psychology, 45,* 279-328.

Simpson, J., Rholes, W., & Nelligan, J. (1992). Support seeking and support giving within couples in an anxiety-provoking situation: The role of attachment styles. *Journal of Personality and Social Psychology, 62,* 434–446.

Skinner, J., Carruth, B., Moran, J., III, Houck, K., Schmidhammer, J., Reed, A., Ott, D. (1998). Toddlers' food preferences: Concordance with family members' preferences. *Journal of Nutrition Education, 30,* 17-22.

Smolak, L., Levine, M., & Schermer, F. (1999). Parental input and weight concerns among elementary school children. *International Journal of Eating Disorders, 25,* 263-271.

Steiger, H., Stotland, S., Trottier, J., & Ghadirian, A. (1996). Familial eating concerns and psychopathological traits: Causal implications of transgenerational effects. *International Journal of Eating Disorders, 19,* 147-157.

Stein, A., & Fairburn, C. (1989). Children of mothers with bulimia nervosa. *British Medical Journal, 299,* 777-778.

Stewart, C., McEwen, F., Konstantellou, A., Eisler, I., & Simic, M. (2017). Impact of ASD traits on treatment outcomes of eating disorders in girls. *European Eating Disorders Review, 25,* 123-128.

Stewart, D., & Robinson, G. (2001). Eating disorders and reproduction. In N. Stotland & D. Stewart (Eds.), *Psychological aspects of women's health care: The interface between psychiatry and obstetrics and gynecology* (2nd ed.) Arlington, VA: American Psychiatric Publishing.

Stiegler, L. (2005). Understanding pica behavior: A review for clinical and education professionals. *Focus on Autism and Other Developmental Disabilities, 20,* 27–38.

Thomas, A., & Chess, S. (1977). *Temperament and development.* New York, NY: Brunner/Mazel.

Thomas, A., Chess, S., & Birch, H. (1970). The origin of personality. *Scientific American, 223,* 102-109.

Torgersen, L., Von Holle, A., Reichborn-Kjennerud, T., Berg, C. K., Hamer, R., Sullivan, P., & Bulik, C. M. (2008). Nausea and vomiting of pregnancy in women with bulimia nervosa and eating disorders not otherwise specified. *The International Journal of Eating Disorders, 41,* 722–727.

Wainstock, T., Lerner-Geva, L., Glasser, S., Shoham-Vardi, I., & Anteby, E. (2013). Prenatal stress and risk of spontaneous abortion. *Psychosomatic Medicine, 75*, 228–235.

Waugh, E., & Bulik, C. M. (1999). Offspring of women with eating disorders. *International Journal of Eating Disorders, 25*, 123-133.

Wertheim, E., Mee, V., & Paxton, S. (1999). Relationships among adolescent girls' eating behaviors and their parents' weight-related attitudes and behaviors. *Sex Roles, 41,* 169-187.

Wiederman, M., & Sansone, R., & Sansone, L. (1998). Disordered eating and perceptions of childhood abuse among women in a primary care setting. *Psychology of Women Quarterly, 22,* 493-497.

Winnicott, D. W. (1987). *The Child, the Family, and the Outside World.* Reading, MA: Perseus Publishing.

Zakin, D. (1989). Eating disturbance, emotional separation, and body image. *International Journal of Eating Disorders, 8,* 411-417.

Zeifman, D. & Hazan, C. (1997). A process model of adult attachment formation. In S. Duck (Ed.), *Handbook of Personal Relationships: Theory, Research and Interventions* (pp. 179–195). John Wiley & Sons Inc.

Zeifman, D. & Hazan, C. (1997). Attachment: The bond in pair-bonds. In J. A. Simpson & D. T. Kenrick (Eds.), *Evolutionary Social Psychology* (pp. 237–263). Lawrence Erlbaum Associates, Inc.

About the Author

Dr. Christina E. Stai, Psy.D., is a licensed clinical psychologist in Iowa and California. She owns a group practice, Holistic Resources LLC, in Southeast Iowa, where she provides individual therapy and neuropsychological assessments for children, teens, and young adults. Dr. Stai specializes in working with people with neurodivergent needs (ADHD, Autism, etc.), trauma and abuse survivors, foster care and adoption, disordered eating concerns, developmental delays, and behavioral and emotional concerns.

Dr. Stai was raised and educated in Southern California. She received her Master's and Doctorate degree in Clinical Psychology from Azusa Pacific University, an APA accredited school. She was trained in a systems-based approach, which emphasizes learning about others within their different systems (family, friends, school, work, faith, etc.). Dr. Stai received Bachelor's degrees in Psychology and Child Development from California State University, Northridge.

Dr. Stai completed an APA accredited internship and APPIC accredited postdoctoral fellowship at Casa Pacifica, a foster care shelter for children. Dr. Stai also completed an assessment practicum at the Center for Autism and Related Disorders (CARD), where she focused on testing, reassessing, and diagnosing children with Autism; and a therapy practicum at BHC Alhambra Hospital in the inpatient eating disorder unit.

Dr. Stai moved to Southeast Iowa in 2015, where she currently resides with her husband, two stepdaughters, and two dogs. In her spare time she enjoys reading, writing, cooking, gardening, and continuing to pursue special interests and education in the field of psychology.

www.ingramcontent.com/pod-product-compliance
Lightning Source LLC
LaVergne TN
LVHW051834080426
835512LV00018B/2881